In Safe Hands

Bullying Prevention with Compassion for All

Sheri Werner

ROWMAN & LITTLEFIELD EDUCATION
A division of
ROWMAN & LITTLEFIELD PUBLISHERS, INC.
Lanham • New York • Toronto • Plymouth, UK

Published by Rowman & Littlefield Education
A division of Rowman & Littlefield Publishers, Inc.
A wholly owned subsidiary of The Rowman & Littlefield Publishing Group, Inc.
4501 Forbes Boulevard, Suite 200, Lanham, Maryland 20706
www.rowman.com

10 Thornbury Road, Plymouth PL6 7PP, United Kingdom

Copyright © 2012 by Sheri Werner

All rights reserved. No part of this book may be reproduced in any form or by any electronic or mechanical means, including information storage and retrieval systems, without written permission from the publisher, except by a reviewer who may quote passages in a review.

British Library Cataloguing in Publication Information Available

Library of Congress Cataloging-in-Publication Data

Werner, Sheri, 1964-
In safe hands : bullying prevention with compassion for all / Sheri Werner.
p. cm.
Includes bibliographical references and index.
ISBN 978-1-61048-809-9 (cloth : alk. paper) -- ISBN 978-1-61048-810-5 (pbk. : alk. paper) -- ISBN 978-1-61048-811-2 (electronic)
1. Bullying in schools--Prevention. I. Title.
LB3013.3.W46 2012
371.5'8--dc23

2012004126

The paper used in this publication meets the minimum requirements of American National Standard for Information Sciences Permanence of Paper for Printed Library Materials, ANSI/NISO Z39.48-1992.

Printed in the United States of America

To all of the students, faculty, staff and families of Foundations School Community for daring to embark upon this unbelievable journey with me…

Contents

Acknowledgements	vii
Preface	ix
Part I — Introduction	1
1 Bullying: A Significant Problem	3
2 Children Who Bully	9
3 Detecting Bullying	13
Part II—What's a Parent to Do?	15
4 Parents Are the Child's Best Advocates	17
5 Why Bully-Proofing Is Unlikely to Work	25
Part III—Helping the Bullies	29
6 Closely Monitoring the Bully	33
7 Creating Opportunities for Bullies to Help Others	39
Part IV—The Connection Factor	47
8 Practicing What We Preach	49
9 Developing a School Anti-bullying Policy	55
Part V — Bullying Prevention in the Classroom	57
10 This Is the Curriculum	59
11 Class Chats: What's Going Well? What's Not?	65
Part VI — Bullying Prevention in the Larger School Community	73

12 Appreciating and Enjoying One Another	75
13 School-Wide Rules and Understandings	83
14 Cyber Bullying and the Role of Schools	101
Part VII—It's a Work in Progress	107
15 Students Speak	115
Appendix 1	123
Appendix 2	127
Appendix 3	131
Appendix 4	135
References	141

Acknowledgements

I would like to thank all of the faculty and staff at Foundations School Community for their dedication and commitment to the critical work of supporting students cognitively, emotionally, and socially at a time when education has become particularly geared toward competition, boosting standardized test scores, and ensuring "cognitive excellence."

I also extend my deepest gratitude to all Foundations School Community parents who were able to "think outside of the box" and to risk seeking something different for their children. I hope you are glad that you did so! I am particularly grateful to all of the students of Foundations School Community, for we could not have done the work we do without you. You have been my greatest teachers!

I want to especially thank Lucy Solomon for holding on to the vision when I couldn't see it, and for supporting me to keep moving forward. Also, to Linda Wysocki, thank you for twenty years of walking with me on this amazing journey, both as a mentor and a friend. And to JoAnne Lange, thank you for your loyalty, dedication, and friendship in working tirelessly with me to build our school.

In addition, I'd like to acknowledge all of my wonderful friends, family members, advocates, and supporters for your presence and ongoing faith and encouragement. I'm sorry I cannot list each of you individually. I hope you realize the impact you each have made on my life.

I'd also like to thank Anne Wayman, my writing coach and editor, who encouraged me to write this book and told me that I actually could do it. To my assistant, Jennifer Balam, who spent countless hours typing this manuscript with great enthusiasm, I am forever grateful.

Lastly, I thank my greatest supporters—my daughters, Kelsi and Alyssa, and especially my husband, Keith—for standing by me through the ups and downs of this wild ride and for always encouraging me to keep moving forward. I love you with all my heart.

Preface

Never doubt that a small group of thoughtful, committed, citizens can change the world. Indeed, it is the only thing that ever has. —Margaret Mead

As an educator (and parent of two) who has been immersed in working tirelessly to create and build a school for the past fifteen years, if someone would have told me that I would be writing a book about bullying prevention, I would have told them that they were sadly mistaken. I would have said that I have more than enough work to do; I am not qualified to write a book, and I have not worked in the field of bullying prevention in schools.

I have since come to realize that I, myself, am the one who is sadly mistaken.

The program introduced in this book was not originally written and developed for use as a "bullying-prevention program," nor was our school created with the conscious intention of preventing bullying or ensuring a "bully-free" environment. I mention this not because I don't believe these are critical aspects of all schools. It's apparent that I do feel this way or I would not have ended up writing this book!

The fact that the program introduced in this book was developed, not in response to the obvious and increasing need for bullying prevention in our schools, but as a model of how all schools may be able to educate children in intellectually, socially, and emotionally safe educational environments, is what differentiates this book from other bullying-prevention books on the market today.

In researching "bullying in schools," one can find hundreds of books, articles, and dissertations written about school bullying, prevention, and intervention. So why would I feel a need to write another one? In further studying the books that have been written, it seems all have been written in response to the increasingly tragic impact that bullying has had on our children, particularly over the past fifteen years. Educators, parents, and health professionals are becoming more aware of the detrimental effects of bullying and are working to develop solutions to address the issue.

Children are now beginning to be viewed as more than just "cognitive beings" who walk through the doors of our classrooms, to be filled with information and then sent home. We are finally starting to acknowledge the need to create better, safer school environments and we are searching for ways to do that.

Many of the books written to date are either academic and technical (research-based), fun and easy to read but not particularly useful, or informative and practical but not explicit enough for parents and educators who want to do the right thing but need step-by-step directions regarding not just what to do to help children (i.e., help children develop social skills), but how to go about doing it.

This book attempts to reach all audiences—educators, parents, mental health professionals, and the community at large—embracing the hope and belief that we can all work together to create safer educational environments for our children.

OUTLINE OF THE BOOK

The book describes how to set up and maintain a school culture that in and of itself fosters a bully-free atmosphere. It is divided into seven parts.

Part I provides an introduction and overview of bullying, including the definition, forms and prevalence of bullying, as well as various reasons children bully. The presentation is not intended to include a comprehensive picture of the full scope of bullying issues, but rather, is confined to my limited research results.

Part II provides a parent education presentation that we developed at Foundations School Community (K–8th grade). It gives detailed information about how parents can connect with and support their children both at home and at school, serving as their advocates. Through the development of strong relationships, parents are able to assist their children in developing a solid sense of self, making them less likely to become victims of bullies or bullies themselves.

Part III consists of various strategies and tools that we have found helpful in supporting children who are actively bullying others. It includes specific techniques and activities for dealing with all aspects of bullying behavior, as well as several real scenarios that we have encountered with bullying. A section addressing various techniques that have been found to be counterproductive in handling bullying behavior is also included.

Part IV describes the necessary training of faculty and staff, which must be included in creating a safe school environment. Examples of activities and discussion topics are included to provide the faculty/staff with tools to develop a meaningful and connected environment. This begins with developing working relationships with one another, in which they can create a school culture that prevents bullying. Also discussed in this section are the crucial components that should be included in a school antibullying policy.

Part V is an overview of the comprehensive classroom curriculum that we created, utilized, and implemented on a daily basis over the past fifteen years. Specific activities and examples are provided to assist with the implementation of these strategies in any school environment.

Part VI focuses on activities to be utilized throughout the larger school community as tools for helping children feel safe and connected, not only to their classmates, but to all students in the school.

This chapter additionally describes a number of school-wide "rules and understandings" that are critical in order to ensure that all students in the school possess knowledge and understanding of the behavioral expectations in their school environment. This section provides information about specific bullying issues that are prevalent at many schools, including issues of sexuality, racial bullying, cyberbullying, exclusion, and bullying of kids with special needs.

Part VII concludes the book, focusing on the need to implement the program slowly, over time, rather than attempting to accomplish too much, too quickly at the risk of not being able to successfully complete the attempted goals.

A discussion about the implementation of the program in larger schools versus smaller schools is addressed, concluding with a section of student interviews and a reminder of the necessity of all educators, parents, and mental health professionals to work together to create cognitively, emotionally, and socially safe schools for our children.

Please note that all the names of children used here are fictitious.

Part I — Introduction

Chapter One

Bullying: A Significant Problem

Since the Columbine tragedy in 1999, the fourth-deadliest school massacre in US history, the issue of bullying and the awareness of the need for bullying-prevention curriculums in our schools has been on the rise. While many schools have attempted to implement various bullying-prevention curriculums, it is difficult to ascertain the effectiveness of these programs.

According to Dr. Ken Rigby, Dan Olweus reported success in the 1980s in a Norway intervention utilizing the "Olweus Bullying Prevention Program," which reduced bullying by 50 percent. However, his intervention method was unable to be replicated outside of Norway.[1]

The most comprehensive review of the success rate of antibullying curriculum claims that the average success rate is 15 percent (Smith, Pepler, and Rigby 2004). Rigby states that success is more likely to be achieved when programs are implemented in the early years, in primary schools, and when the programs are applied thoroughly—meaning all faculty, students, and other community members are involved in the implementation of the program.

Although it is tragic that we seem to have a looming and desperate need to address the bullying that occurs in our schools, clearly the need exists. In 2010 statistics estimated that 160,000 children miss school every day due to fear of bullies.[2] American schools are also believed to harbor 2.1 million bullies and 2.7 million of their victims.[3]

Additionally, suicide remains among the leading cause of death of children under fourteen years old. A review of students from thirteen countries found signs of connection between bullying, being bullied, and suicide in children.[4]

This connection has been shockingly illuminated recently in the suicide deaths of several youths as a result of bullying in the United States. It is difficult to ascertain the number of children who commit suicide each year due to bullying, as other factors including anxiety and depression may be a contributing factor to the suicide.

Although there are approximately about fifteen to twenty-five reported incidents of bullying suicide each year, there may be substantially more than that if we include those incidences that are not primarily attributed to bullying and incidents that are unreported.[5]

It is only recently, however, with students becoming more willing to report episodes of bullying and the tragedies associated with its effect, that bullying has begun to receive serious research attention within the scientific community.

According to studies conducted by the National Center for Education Statistics (NCES) in 2003, 2005, and 2007, only 7.1 percent of students aged twelve to eighteen reported being bullied in 2003. In 2005, that number jumped to 28.1 percent and in 2007 it increased to a significant 31.7 percent. That is a tragic 24.6 percent increase in less than ten years.[6]

This increase of reporting is likely due to the fact that society is now more aware of bullying and its devastating effects, due to the increased media attention focused on the deaths of youth who were victims of bullying.[7]

As public awareness in countries around the world has increased along with a rise in publicity about mass homicides and suicides by those who feel hopeless, students have perhaps begun to feel less isolated and more willing to talk about bullying as it relates to themselves and their peers.

Due to this increased research focus and attention, our understanding of the complexity, significance, and scope of school bullying has grown dramatically over the past twenty years. Yet, despite this significant focus and attention, bullying continues to plague our society and our schools.

There are several reasons for this:

1. *Difficulty in detecting bullying.* Bullies can be sly and insidious. Hence, they don't bully when others can see, especially when adults are around. As a result, they often don't get caught bullying.
2. *Victims don't tell.* Because victims of bullying are often fearful of retribution or making their situation worse than it already is, many won't report being bullied.
3. *Bystanders don't intervene.* Children who see another child being bullied often will not step in to help or tell an adult, for fear that they will be the next target of the bully.
4. *Adults don't understand what they're seeing.* Many adults simply are unaware of the signs and symptoms of bullying or they chalk it up to "kids being kids."

5. *Aware adults lack resources.* Adults who see a child being bullied may stop it in the moment but often do not know how to facilitate or support a long-term solution.
6. *Lack of effective programs.* There are not enough school-wide programs being implemented to effectively educate administrators, teachers, and parents about bullying and how to deal with it both in and outside of school. There are even fewer programs designed to garner community support for stopping bullying or that focus on creating environments that ensure students cognitive, emotional, and social safety.

DEFINITION OF BULLYING

The definition of bullying has been examined and debated in the research literature over the years. Indeed, bullying behavior has been described in a wide variety of different ways, including, but not limited to:

- Aggression
- The systematic abuse of power
- An intentional desire of one or more people to hurt another person
- An ongoing repeated attack—physical, psychological, social, or verbal—on those who are powerless to resist
- Continual physical, psychological, social, verbal, or emotional method of intimidating a person

Dan Olweus provides us with a commonly accepted definition for bullying in his book, *Bullying at School: What We Know and What We Can Do* (1993). For the purpose of this book, we will use his definition of bullying, which is: "A person is bullied when he or she is exposed repeatedly and over time, to negative actions on the part of one or more other persons, and he or she has difficulty defending himself or herself."[8]

Simply stated, *when a person intentionally inflicts psychological or physical pain on another person, that person is bullying.* The perpetrators are physically or psychologically more potent than their victims. This does NOT mean that the perpetrators are necessarily physically or psychologically stronger in reality, even though they are almost always portrayed as larger or stronger by all involved parties.

Forms of Bullying

One of the difficulties in detecting and dealing with bullying behaviors is that bullying takes place in many different ways, some of which can be difficult to detect. The following are several types of bullying to be aware of:

1. Emotional bullying: This type of bullying can be very subtle. It includes gossiping, spreading rumors, excluding others from activities, certain looks and eye contact, isolating or shunning someone, or anything else that causes another person emotional pain.
2. Physical bullying: This type of bullying involves any type of physically harmful behavior, including hitting, kicking, pushing, hair pulling, or even threatening physical harm.
3. Verbal bullying: This type of bullying includes teasing, mocking, taunting, insulting, laughing at someone, and verbally assaulting another person in any way.
4. Racist bullying: This type of bullying includes any type of racial or ethnic comment, slur, offensive gesture, or making fun of someone's cultural traditions.
5. Religious bullying: This type of bullying is similar to racist bullying and includes any type of slur or disparagement of someone's faith. It includes negative comments about things such as religious medals or special apparel.
6. Sexual bullying: This type of bullying includes sexual harassment of any kind, including jokes, comments, teasing, or taunting about sexual body parts, teasing about gender identity or sexual orientation, starting rumors about sexual activities, and/or any unwanted physical contact.
7. Cyber bullying: This type of bullying includes harassment by sending or posting hurtful images or messages or threats via e-mail, instant messaging, Internet chat rooms, social media sites, text messages, by cell phone or other computer. This type of bullying is difficult to detect because it allows for anonymity. It should be noted that cyber bullying often includes one or more of the other types of bullying.

Prevalence of Bullying

Estimates of the prevalence of bullying are difficult to determine because they depend a great deal upon both the definitions and research methods that are employed by the investigators. Consequently, these estimates tend to be time-based, momentary snapshots of bullying occurrence.

For our purposes, we will use the startling conclusion that in most schools, one in five pupils has suffered from a broad range of bullying and one in ten confesses in anonymous questionnaires to have actively bullied others (Lines 2008). This means that 20 percent of our children are being bullied on a regular basis and 10 percent of our children are bullies.

It is also commonplace for students to move among the roles of bully, victim, bully-victim, and bystander (Swearer Espelage, and Napolitano 2009). According to the National Association of School Psychologists, physical bullying increases in elementary school, peaks in middle school, and declines in high school. However, although direct, physical bullying seems to decrease with age, verbal bullying seems to remain constant regardless of the age group.[9]

NOTES

1. "Bullying in Schools and What to Do About It." 2010. KenRigby.net.
2. "Stop Bullying Harassment and Violence." 2010. www.bullyingstatistics.org.
3. "Make a Sound for a Voice Unheard." 2009. www.makebeatsnotbeatdowns.org.
4. "Bullying Suicide Link Explored in New Study by Researchers at Yale." 2008. opac.yale.edu.
5. "Bullying Suicide Statistics—Bullycide—Teen Depression." www.teendepression.org/stats/bullying-suicide-statistics-bullycide/.
6. www.students.com.miami.edu/netreporting.
7. Shelley Hymel and Susan Swearer, "Bullying: An Age-old Problem That Needs New Solutions." education.com.www.education.com/reference/article/bullying-about-power-and-abuse-of-power/.
8. "What Is Bullying?" Olweus Bullying Prevention Program. www.olweus.org/public/bullying.page.
9. powerfulfamilies.org.

Chapter Two

Children Who Bully

Almost everyone who has ever thought about how often and how many children are involved in bullying ask, "Why do kids bully?" There is no universal answer to this question. Each child has individual reasons for bullying other children, but there is some commonality. The following are some of the more common causes of bullying behavior:

- *Abusive or Aggressive Behavior in the Home.* If a child lives in a home where family members are insensitive to one another, have difficulty communicating and sharing feelings, lack affection, and/or witness a culture of physical violence, this can be very disturbing to a child.

One of the results is that the child acts out by bullying peers. Gerald Patterson has conducted research into aggression and child-rearing practices for the past thirty-five years. J. Hoover and R. Oliver (1996) refer to his research, saying:

> According to Patterson's research, child-rearing practices that are associated with the development of aggression include harsh and inconsistent disciplinary practices, limited parental involvement, and a failure to provide adequate supervision (pg 13).

- *Desire to Gain Power and Popularity.* Bullies are generally, though not always, bigger and stronger than their victims and use intimidation to get what they want. They often enjoy the feeling of being powerful and in charge of the situation to the extent that "power makes them feel good about themselves."[1]

At our school we saw this in nine-year-old Hannah, who was clearly the alpha-female of the third grade class.

Hannah was physically bigger and stronger than the other girls her age and very well-spoken; children looked up to her and often followed her lead. When Hannah decided that the third-grade girls should be mean to all the second-grade girls by excluding them from games and not talking to them on the playground, several third-grade girls joined Hannah in this endeavor.

Fortunately, the teachers caught on quickly and the issue was addressed immediately. However, in this example, Hannah clearly attempted to empower herself at the expense of making others feel intimidated and excluded.

- *Feelings of Anger, Hurt, and Fear.* When children feel angry, hurt, or fearful they are more likely to act these feelings out on those they can dominate.

In another example from our school, ten-year-old Henry was constantly teasing a younger boy. When the issue was being addressed in class, Henry broke down in tears, stating that he knew he shouldn't tease kids and admitted that he was constantly being teased at home by two older brothers and that he hated it. It is helpful to remind children that when people act out against others it is often because they are feeling badly themselves.

This does not excuse the acting-out behavior, but it helps children to remember that the person who is inflicting the hurt onto others is also in need of help. In other words, we must stop the bullies from hurting others and then try to help them with their own feelings of anger, hurt, or fear, which are causing them to act out against other people.

There are many reasons that children feel angry, hurt, or fearful and as a result transfer these feelings to bullying behaviors. Here are some of the more common reasons:

- They are victims of bullying at school or at home (by siblings, parents, or caregivers).
- They have problems in some area of their lives and thus feel inadequate (i.e., learning issues, body image struggles, poor social skills, low self-esteem, etc.). Bullying makes them feel as if they have power and control over some area of their lives.
- They feel neglected by parents, teachers, or peers and are looking for attention. The negative attention they get from bullying is better than no attention at all.

THE SITUATIONAL BULLY

While some kids will bully at all times in every situation, other children may only be bullies in situations when they feel they have no other option.

For example, second-grader Ken didn't want to sit next to Rob at recess and lunch because Rob always asked Ken to trade food, which was very disturbing to Ken. Rather than tell Rob he didn't want to share food, Ken began to tell Rob that Rob wasn't allowed to sit at that table when he approached Ken every day. Rob was very upset and couldn't figure out why Ken wouldn't let him sit at the table.

Ken turned to bullying behavior because he didn't know how to express his feelings openly by telling Rob that he didn't want to share his food.

Children who would not ordinarily bully may also do so if something traumatic is happening in their lives, like the death of a relative or pet, the birth of a sibling, a divorce, moving, and so on. Bullying is their way of acting out their distress over the upsetting situation they are experiencing.

It is very important to help children understand that regardless of what they, or any other people, are experiencing in any area of their lives, there is never a reason or an excuse to treat another person badly. This is a message that parents can learn to start teaching children in their home from the time their children are very small.

School administrators and teachers and any other adults involved at school must constantly make it clear that there is NO reason that merits bullying behavior.

NOTE

1. www.child-discipline-with-love.com/why-do-children-bully.html.

Chapter Three

Detecting Bullying

While physical bullying can be easier to detect because it often results in noticeable harm to a child's body, such harm can be hidden. Emotional bullying can be even more difficult to detect. More importantly however, whether the damage is physical or emotional, children who are being bullied are unlikely to tell anyone that this is happening. In addition to being fearful of being labeled a "tattletale" or a "snitch" by other students and of possibly having the bully retaliate if they tell an adult, children also feel helpless. Since they are not able to see their way out of it, they don't believe anyone else can or will be able to help them either.

Barbara Coloroso in her book, *The Bully, the Bullied, and the Bystander*, claims that more children have also "bought into the lie that bullying is a necessary part of growing up. It might hurt like hell, but the hell is part of the landscape of childhood" (Coloroso 2008, pg. 49). She states that children may believe that some adults are included in the lie because there are some adults in their lives who bully them too, and so adults are somehow sanctioning this bullying behavior.

In a school environment, teachers often have a hard time recognizing emotional bullying, name calling, ostracizing, exclusion, spreading rumors, and racial or sexual taunts because the bullies are so good at making sure no teacher or other adult hears what's going on. If a child complains, it becomes one child's word against the other's and the teacher or other adult has no real way to sort it out.

Here's how one expert describes this impasse:

> Victims of emotional bullying may find it tough to talk about their experiences. They may be paralysed with fear, or just accustomed to keeping their worries to themselves. It's very difficult to catch the perpetrator red-handed and it is most likely that the victim will be told to 'get over it,' 'find somewhere else to play,' or 'stop telling tales.' (Milburn-Curtis 2007, pg. 27)

Of course, admonitions to "stop telling tales" or "go find somewhere else to play" mean the child who is reporting being bullied is not heard and the bully is likely to do even harsher bullying as payback for tattling. Everyone loses with this approach.

Children often don't want to tell the teacher that they are being bullied because they fear the consequences, and thus will try to figure out ways to handle the situation on their own or they will try to avoid the bully at school.

At home, children may also be reluctant to tell their parents they are being emotionally bullied at school. They may be afraid their parents will insist that the child do something about it, such as talk to a teacher or administrator. Sometimes the parents themselves will decide to go talk to someone at the school which causes their child to fear that disclosure will only worsen the situation.

At school and at home it's usually up to the adults to determine when a child is being bullied. The symptoms of being bullied that a child may display are:

- Becoming moody or short tempered.
- Finding excuses for not wanting to go to school.
- Claiming physical illnesses such as stomachaches and headaches that may have, in fact, actually evolved into such physical symptoms.
- Returning to bedwetting.
- Beginning to have nightmares.
- Developing either a lack of appetite or increase of eating compulsively.
- Having difficulty concentrating.
- Deterioration in the quality of schoolwork.
- Having insomnia, anxiety.
- Starting to become quiet, withdrawn.
- Exhibiting physical signs like bruises, torn clothing, scrapes, and so on.
- Expressing sadness and/or violence in writing or drawings.
- Displaying unusual acting out behaviors.

Part II — What's a Parent to Do?

Supporting children with their daily struggles can be challenging enough without the added stress of having to help them negotiate issues of bullying. Watching children endure the pain that bullying causes brings a great deal of distress to parents as well as to their children.

It can be difficult for parents to support their child because their own feelings of anger, hurt, denial, fear, and guilt get in the way of being able to think clearly and face the issues at hand.

If parents expect to effectively support their children in dealing with issues of bullying, it is critical that they deal with the variety of feelings it inevitably brings up for them to see their child being physically, mentally, or emotionally hurt in any way.

The following are some ways for parents to get support for themselves so that they can be fully present to support their children:

- *Become informed.* Read books, pamphlets, and educational materials. Find out all that you can about bullying and what you can do to help your child. This will help you to realize that you and your child are not alone and that it is not your (or your child's) fault that this is happening.
- *Attend lectures/workshops on bullying to acquire more knowledge/resources.* Knowledge is an empowering step in the process of helping yourself and your child. You will begin to meet other parents in the same position you're in as well as experts and other people such as school administrators and faculty to connect with and share information.
- *Individual counseling/therapy.* Talking about and sharing your experience and feelings with a professional will help! This is a great way to deal with feelings of anger, guilt, hopelessness, or any other emotions that get in the way of you being effective in helping your child.

- *Group counseling/therapy/support.* There are various support groups for people who have experienced what you are going through. Sharing your experience with others who understand can be very beneficial in helping you realize that you are not alone and that there is help and hope.
- *Form your own support group.* If you can't find a system of support that already exists, it is fairly easy to set up an informal group consisting of parents who wish to support one another around bullying and perhaps other issues that parents struggle with. Meeting once or twice a month will help more than you know.

Chapter Four

Parents Are the Child's Best Advocates

While parents cannot guarantee that their children will never experience difficult and painful interactions with other children in their school environment, parents should absolutely be able to feel that their children will be physically and emotionally safe at school at all times.

There are many things parents can do to support their children in experiencing a bully-free education in a school environment.

Nobody in the world is more invested in the health, safety, happiness, and well-being of children than their parents. The relationship between a parent and child is like no other. As parents, we have an instinctive need and desire to care for and to protect our children. We love our children intensely and spend an enormous amount of time and resources caring for their physical, emotional, and mental well-being.

Parents also know their children better than anyone else. These factors make parents the best and most important advocates for their children. As such, parents must remain connected to their children and their children's emotional, social, and cognitive lives.

It is easy as our children get older and more independent to lose that day-to-day connection that occurred so naturally in their early years, (ages zero to six) when your children relied on you heavily to help meet their daily needs in all areas of their lives. With their growing independence, it's easy to slip into a physical and emotional detachment that includes less daily contact, play, less one-on-one time, and less communication with parents.

Although this is normal, it presents a challenge because it is through these types of interactions with your children that you are able to remain connected in their lives. Staying connected to your children, regardless of outside factors, is the most critical component of being able to assist them with issues of bullying, or with any other problem they encounter.

The stronger their relationship with you is, the more likely it is they will come to you when they need help or are in distress.

The following are some suggestions of ways to connect and stay connected with your children:

SPECIAL TIME

Special Time is very important and is a great way to develop and maintain closeness with your children from the time they are young all the way through their teenage years.

"Special Time," as described by Patty Wipfler (1990), Founder of "Hand in Hand Parenting," consists of a parent spending a well-defined amount of one-on-one time with his or her child. This time must be uninterrupted and the focus of the parent's attention is solely on the child.

The child completely controls the play and the parent follows the child's lead. During Special Time, the parent tries to remain pleased and does not try to teach, advise, or control the child, unless there is an issue of safety.

Examples of special time activities for younger children (two to ten years) may include:

- Wrestling
- Role-playing (school, house, tea parties, etc.)
- Playing with dolls, Barbies, and so on
- Building with Legos or other materials
- Playing chase games, water play
- Playing board games

Examples of special time activities for older children ten to eighteen years may include:

- Playing board games
- Getting your hair/nails done
- Going for a walk
- Building something together
- Flying a kite
- Going out to lunch
- Going to a movie
- Going to the mall
- Any type of physical play

A great benefit of special time is that it often assists parents in understanding problems that their children are struggling with. Younger children often choose to play games that depict issues in their lives that they are trying to process.

For instance, five-year-old Helen regularly had special time with her mom. One summer before her kindergarten year, Helen's special-time sessions became more solely focused on playing school. During these times, Helen would be the teacher and make her mom be the student.

Helen would tell her mom to read a book and then make her mom say, "I don't know how to read yet."

Then Helen would yell at her mom for not being able to read.

This happened several times and led to a discussion where Helen was able to express her worry about expectations at kindergarten. She was able to talk with her mom about whether she was ready to meet those expectations and what would happen to her if she wasn't.

Helen's brother had attended our school for several years and Helen was aware that children were not expected to know how to read in kindergarten; she also knew that children were never yelled at there. Nonetheless, she had internalized this fear. Fortunately, her mom was able to help Helen process these feelings and deal with her fears through their special-time play.

SPENDING TIME AS A FAMILY

While special time is more focused on one-on-one time with your child, spending time with your child as a family is also very important. As you spend family time, you develop a family bond, fun memories, and closeness.

In today's world of advanced technology, it can be quite difficult to simply spend time with our children without the distraction of cell phones, iPods, computers, video games, and so on. Nonetheless, we must! We have to put our devices away, demand that they put theirs away too and take some time to just be together.

Here are some ideas of things you can do together:

- *Family Dinner.* Go around the table during dinner time and have each person say the best part of their day (and the worst if you want).
- *Family Community Service.* The family chooses a community service project to do together. Each family member can have a turn choosing a different project.
- *Family Game Night.* Take turns choosing a game to play together.
- *Family Vacations and/or Camping Trips.* Great fun and helps build wonderful memories together!

- *Family Day Trips.* Each member of the family gets a turn to decide where you will go for a weekly or monthly day trip.
- *Family Cleaning Days.* The family takes on a cleaning project together that benefits your home (i.e., cleaning out the garage, the yard, closets, etc.).
- *Movie Night.* The family watches a movie together once per week or month, either at home or at a theater or both. Everyone takes a turn choosing the movie.

FAMILY MEETINGS

Similar to classroom chats where children discuss what is going well in the class and what is not going well, it is important that families get together regularly for a family meeting to discuss how things are going in the family.

The following guidelines (which are similar to classroom chat guidelines) will help the family to facilitate an effective and productive discussion:

- One family member speaks at a time.
- Each member of the family listens thoughtfully and with an open mind when someone else is speaking.
- When it's your turn to speak, speak about your own thoughts, feelings, and opinions in a respectful manner.
- Do not comment, either positively or negatively, on someone else's thoughts, feelings, and opinions.
- Do not give people advice.
- Be respectful of opinions that are different from your own.

The family meeting should begin with each member of the family taking a turn stating something they feel is going well within the family system. Beginning with positive things helps people to remember that positive things are happening within the family even if there are some difficulties or problems occurring as well.

After the good things are shared, problems can be discussed. There should be an agreement to discuss a limited number of problems per meeting, depending on time constraints and the number of problems there are to discuss.

It is helpful to end the family meeting by having each person say something they appreciate about the person sitting to their right (or left) and something they appreciate about themselves. (See Birthday Appreciation Circles.)

SPECIAL INTERESTS

As your children grow, they will develop various interests about all sorts of fascinating subjects. From the latest video games through retro dolls, and of course the hottest media figures and singing groups . . . your children's various interests will intrigue and baffle you. What is your role? What they are interested in, you need to be interested in!

Start gathering information on the latest kid's fad. Really getting familiar with your child's interests is an excellent way of connecting with your child. You want to be able to discuss and participate (at some level) in their interests with them.

We once had a parent whose child was at our school from kindergarten through eighth grade. When his daughter graduated and moved on to high school, she began dyeing her hair, piercing her body, and listening to all kinds of outrageous music. At least, he found the music outrageous. The father was a conservative attorney, who fortunately wanted to remain close to his daughter. He decided to buy two tickets to a concert of a rock band that he knew she liked.

I'll never forget this clean-cut conservative guy describing his experience at what turned out to be a rave.

He'd accompanied his daughter in his business suit as she sported her mini skirt, black boots, and tube top. When he found himself shielding his sixteen-year-old in the middle of the mosh-pit midway through the concert, he wondered if perhaps this father–daughter bonding idea was not all it was cracked up to be! Later on, of course, it paid real dividends for both of them.

Something to keep in mind in the midst of whatever activity you find yourself engaged in with or because of your children is that the more connected you are with your children, the more likely it is that your children will confide in you if they are being bullied or experiencing other difficulties at school or in other areas of their lives.

Furthermore, through your connection with your children, you will be able to determine whether they are experiencing challenges in their daily lives that they may not be talking to you about.

Another important reason to remain closely connected to your children is because children who feel connected to their parents and who are given regular positive attention by loving parents are less likely to bully other children or to allow themselves to be in a situation to be bullied or treated poorly by others.

WHAT PARENTS CAN ACTUALLY DO

Although parents cannot protect their children from every hurtful situation, in addition to developing strong connections with their children as discussed above, there are several skills and tools that parents can teach their children which will help children deal with many issues in life. In addition, there are specific steps parents can take to ensure that their children are not the victims of bullying.

Model Value-Based Social Skills

One of the most important things parents could do about bullies is to teach and model value-based social skills and coping strategies at home from the time their children are very young.[1] These skills include socially acceptable and desirable characteristics, which are valued in the home as well as at school.

Although such skills are a book in themselves, here is a list that pretty much sums up their essence:

- Respect of one another (and one another's belongings)
- Appropriate sharing and listening to one another's feelings (using words, not hitting, etc.)
- Healthy expressions of anger, hurt, sadness, and other feelings
- Sharing skills—how and why do we share?
- Importance of working together (collaboration)—(i.e., clean-up time, helping friends, waiting our turn, etc.)
- Problem-solving skills
- Responsibility for belongings, behavior, and actions
- Honesty in all interactions/relationships

As children experience these skills modeled from an early age, these behaviors will become natural to them. If these skills were not modeled in your home, there is still hope as it is never too late to begin practicing value-based social skills in any environment.

Another helpful approach is to enroll your child in a developmental preschool that is focused on the socialization of children and on supporting children through the implementation of an experience-based curriculum, which includes the incorporation of many of the above-mentioned value-based social skills.

There are, of course, many other things you can do, including:

- *Play dates.* It is important to help your children develop relationships with their peers. Play dates are a great way to do this. Be sure to monitor the play dates to ensure the children are playing appropriately and that someone is there to help the children in a thoughtful manner if and when they encounter problems or disagreements.

  It is critical that you help encourage and support your children's social relationships throughout their school experience. It's also critical to keep in mind that regardless of what is going well or poorly at school, having close relationships with even a couple of friends will help a child who is struggling or experiencing difficulty at school.
- *Make sure your child is engaged in activities outside of school.* Every child should be involved in at least one activity or group like team sports, art class, a religious group, a drama club, Boy/Girl Scouts, and so on.

  Having groups and/or activities outside of school will assist children in making friends with peers from different schools. As a result, a child who is experiencing difficulties with children at school will have an opportunity to feel successful in an alternative environment.

  Having at least one outlet where a child feels connected to other children is critical and can make the difference between a child feeling isolated and rejected or feeling accepted, at least somewhere, amongst peers.
- *Do your homework before enrolling your child in an elementary school.* Ask questions about how the school handles bullying and other forms of teasing and emotionally/physically hurtful behavior. How do they handle discipline? Do they have an antibullying program in place? If so, what is it and how is it implemented?

  Many schools say they have a "no tolerance" for bullying policy. What does this actually mean? Does that mean that a child gets kicked out of school for teasing another child, or just for beating up another child? How does their policy, whatever it is, help children to learn acceptance and tolerance so that they can find a place of meeting one another on common ground?

  Ask the difficult questions. Ask other parents, and students too, about their experience at the school. If you are not satisfied with the answers, find another school. If your child is attending the local public school, you can look into transferring him to another nearby public school, if you are unable to move or make other school arrangements.

  If this is not feasible, and your child must attend a school that you don't feel has a satisfactory bullying-prevention program in place, then you must become proactive in helping your child. (See the next section.)

NOTE

1. "3 Steps to Bully-Proof Your Kid." familyfirst.com/3-steps-to-bully-proof-your-kid.html.

Chapter Five

Why Bully-Proofing Is Unlikely to Work

Researchers have suggested many ways to "bully-proof" children. Some of the more common ways include teaching children to:

- Ignore the bully's verbal abuse.
- Try to make friends with the bully.
- Try to reason with the bully.
- Stand up to the bully.
- Laugh at the bully.
- Walk away from the bully.
- Tell an adult.
- Take a self-defense class.

While these well-meaning strategies may be helpful at certain times in specific situations, they lack the depth and continuity to address the complexity of the bullying issue over time. Walking away from a bully, for example, might be helpful on one given day, but may not work the next, nor does it help the bully or the bullied student address the ongoing issue between them.

Making friends with the bully may work as long as the bullied child is willing to go along with whatever the bully wants her to do, but she may find herself the target of the bully once again when she tries to disagree with the bully or the bully's behavior.

Chapter 5

HELPING YOUR BULLIED CHILD

If your child is already enrolled in a school and is experiencing bullying, here are some ways you can get involved in the school and proactively make a difference, or at the very least, help your own child:

- *Determine if the bullying is physical or verbal.* Depending on which it is, decide whether your child can speak to a teacher or administrator on his own or if it will work better if you accompany him.
- *If there is not an antibullying program in place at the school, speak to an administrator about starting one.* Offer to help, in any way you can, to get a program started immediately in the school. One of the easiest ways is to bring in a known program or expert who can help the school implement a program.
- *Offer to support your child's school by volunteering.* You might, for example, be able to assist in your child's classroom and/or to help the school by fundraising, or by watering plants, making copies, or doing whatever else is needed. It has been said, "If you are a supportive, reliable parent teachers will naturally take you seriously when you raise concerns about school safety."[1]

   Furthermore, the more time you spend on campus, the more you will be able to learn about the social/emotional climate of the school.
- *If all else fails, remove your child from the school.* If you seek help and over a period of time the problem is not sufficiently and continuously addressed and monitored, and as a result your child does not feel physically or emotionally safe at school, remove your child from the school.

   Many parents leave their children in school environments where they are clearly suffering emotionally, or even physically, with the hope that it will get better.

   If the school does not have an effective, consistent antibullying program in place, where children are being held accountable for their behavior, then the bullying will not stop and things will not get better for your child.

   Your child may stop talking about it with you after a while because she doesn't want the embarrassment of having you involved, but bullying behaviors don't just stop without intervention.
- *If another child physically harms your child at school, you should report that child to the school authorities.* Depending on the level of physical threat or harm to your child, you may also report the other child to the police so that that child does not harm other children.

As difficult as it is for parents to find themselves in the position of encountering the issue of bullying in the life of their children, parents, as a result of their deep love and commitment to their children, are in the very best position to help both prevent bullying and to assist their children if they are bullied.

Nobody will help, love, and care for the needs of your child the way that you do. Don't hesitate to step up and take whatever action is necessary. Your child's present and future is at stake.

NOTE

1. "Bullying In Schools: Recognizing School Bullying." learningdisabilities.about.com.

Part III—Helping the Bullies

It's important to help children who are bullying others because these children are often hurting as badly as their victims. As bullies are often viewed in a negative light due to their behavior, it is easy to overlook the fact that they also need attention and intervention.

The fact that bullies often appear confident, manipulative, and insensitive makes it challenging to empathize with them. Bullies also often exhibit bravado, making it appear that they are aware of and in control of their actions.

As parents and educators, we cannot let these behaviors and actions fool us. Nor can we ignore bullying or attribute it to "normal childhood behavior" or a "stage the child is going through" that will pass.

It is not normal to hurt other people. It is not normal for children to hurt each other.

Furthermore, if children are hurting others and getting away with it, they will likely continue this behavior. As a human being and educator, I believe and recommend that we adopt the premise that all children are naturally good people.

All children want to love others, be loved by others, to contribute positively to their families and to the community, and they want to feel needed and important in their lives. Children who behave in a contrary fashion do so because they are feeling upset and badly about themselves.

If we can understand and embrace that premise, then we can help these children to change. I have seen a number of children change their behavior when they receive the type of support discussed in this section.

Keep in mind that it is a lot easier to prevent children from becoming bullies by implementing the actions discussed throughout this book than it is to intervene with children who are already bullying others. By the time children become bullies, they are already feeling angry, hurt, sad, powerless, hopeless, invincible, or any combination of these emotions.

Nonetheless, regardless of when and how children become bullies, the reality is that we must intervene to help these children in order to prevent them from committing additional and continuous acts of bullying against others.

One of the great aspects of designing a school curriculum that includes bullying prevention from the early years is that it creates a culture of socially and emotionally aware students.

Hence, if new students enter the school and attempt to bully others, their peers immediately recognize their behavior as negative; the children also immediately understand that the bullies need some help.

A couple of years ago, for example, Darren transferred to our sixth grade from a large public school. For about his first week at our school he was quiet and nice to other students. After the first week, Darren became argumentative with the other children.

It turned out he did not know how to communicate or play with other students in a respectful manner. He called the other students names, claiming he was just joking; he argued constantly when things didn't go his way, and became physical with his peers on several occasions.

During his second week of school, Darren became upset with the boy he perceived as the alpha-male in his class and he challenged that boy to a fight after school. The boy, Bill, had spent all of his school years at our school. He actually thought that the fight was a game of sorts and that it might be something new and fun to try. Consequently, Bill agreed to the after-school meeting.

Fortunately, all of the students began discussing this impending fight and the teachers intervened before it was able to occur.

When we spoke to Darren about challenging Bill to a fight, Darren merely shrugged it off. He explained to us that these fights occurred daily at his old school and nobody really cared.

He stated that when kids don't get along or they strongly disagreed, it is standard practice, from his experience, to "fight it out." We explained to Darren that at our school we do not tolerate fighting or disrespecting students in any way. We also let him know that other students would not be permitted to harm or disrespect him either.

I wish I could say that things got easier with Darren after that. However, that was not the case. Although we saw some improvement in his actions, it continued to be a work in progress to teach, model, and modify Darren's behavior.

We have had many students like Darren who enter our school in their later school years who have already developed the traits and actions of a bully. The process with these students, as it was with Darren, is long and slow, and requires a great amount of patience and tolerance on the part of other students as well as the faculty and staff.

The first order of business with these students is to let the bullies know that we are happy to have them at our school and that although they are not used to the way things are done in our environment, we are going to work hard to help them feel safe, make friends, and become productive members of our school community.

Inevitably when we ask students if they want our help, they will initially respond that they do not want our support. Many children who bully are hurt and angry and they don't trust that the adults can help them.

We explain to these students that all children want to have friends and that we are committed to the process of helping them find some. After denying that they want friends and claiming they don't care about the other kids, once these children realize that the adults are sincere about our commitment to helping them, they always concede to the fact that they do want friends and that they want our help.

Bullies are often simply not convinced that prosocial behavior will help them attain the things they want to achieve. They need to find out that they can be successful in their relationships with others without bullying and that they, themselves, have control over that success.

In our work with children who bully, we have found the following strategies to be helpful:

- Closely monitor the bullies, intervening as quickly as possible when you see or hear that they are harming another child in any way.
- Implement natural consequences for the bully's behavior.
- Engage the bully's peers in helping.
- Model respectful, peaceful, and thoughtful communication as a means of teaching problem-solving skills and empathy.
- Designate an adult to serve as a mentor to the bully.
- Provide positive feedback to bullies regarding their actions that are thoughtful, respectful, and kind. (Remember to ask them how those actions made them feel.)
- Create opportunities for bullies to help others both inside and outside of the school community.
- Have an administrator meet with the bully and the bully's parents.
- Use humor and have fun!

Chapter Six

Closely Monitoring the Bully

At home or in school, children who are known to bully others must be monitored closely. This monitoring is critical for the protection of others as well as for the bully. Naturally, we do not want children harming other children; at the same time, the continuous act of bullying also further harms the bully and makes it more difficult for him to form positive relationships with others.

Bullying can be insidious and often difficult to detect. By closely monitoring the bully, especially during times when there is increased contact with others (recess and lunch period), an adult can intervene and offer assistance before the situation escalates.

It is much easier to prevent bullying than it is to repair the damage inflicted by a bully. Closely monitoring students who are known to bully others also provides a feeling of safety for all students by showing that bullying prevention is a priority and bullying will not be tolerated.

NATURAL CONSEQUENCES

Later in the book I explain the concept and value of natural consequences. In short, a natural consequence is something that occurs naturally as a result of a certain action. For example, if I bump my head (the action) then it will hurt (the consequence).

Bullies must be held accountable for their behavior, and they often are not. The result is they get away with harming others, which further harms them as well. This creates a vicious cycle where bullies continue to act out on others, feel badly about themselves (in some cases) for harming others, see that they can get away with this behavior, and repeat their actions because nothing is stopping them from doing so.

Bullies must be stopped in their tracks, told very clearly (but not disrespectfully) that their behavior is unacceptable, provided with the tools and venues to take ownership of this behavior, and allowed the opportunity to responsibly deal with the situation in whatever manner is appropriate.

Take, for example, Elaine. She was a very angry young girl when she came to our school as a preteen and had to be constantly monitored as she often picked on other students.

One day another girl in her class was missing her CD player. The girl, Susan, was crying as she made an announcement to the class that her CD player was missing.

Everyone speculated what could have happened to it. Someone stated that she saw Elaine holding it, and Elaine quickly denied ever seeing the CD player. Other students tried to offer suggestions about what may have happened to it. Susan continued to cry as she explained where she left it and when she last remembered having it.

A few minutes later, Jed walked into the classroom, arriving thirty minutes late for school. I was teaching that class at the time, so I quickly explained to Jed that we were in the middle of a discussion about Susan's missing CD player.

Without missing a beat, Jed replied, "Oh, you mean the CD player I saw Elaine put in her backpack yesterday?" Everyone froze and looked at Elaine. At that point Elaine admitted taking Susan's CD player.

It was an uncomfortable time for everyone in that sixth-grade classroom. Nonetheless, as this was a critical issue and an ideal learning opportunity, I quickly decided to scrap math and allow students the opportunity to discuss this situation.

Obviously all of the students were very angry, and Elaine was quite uncomfortable. I began by acknowledging to the class that this was a very upsetting situation and everyone would have the opportunity to share their thoughts and feelings.

I also reminded them that although Elaine made a bad choice and committed an unacceptable act, that she was not a bad person and she was still a member of our classroom community. I explained further that our thoughts and feelings must be shared in a respectful manner, without accusing, blaming, or making hurtful comments.

I then asked Susan to talk about how she felt knowing that Elaine had taken her CD player. It is important for bullies to hear, see, and understand how their behavior affects others. Next, I allowed Elaine to respond to Susan's thoughts and feelings. Elaine, who obviously felt badly, apologized and explained that she was not sure why she had taken the CD player; she also shared that initially she just couldn't admit to taking it.

Others then had a chance to share their feelings. The conversation was even more difficult when it shifted to include a discussion of Elaine's general behavior toward many of her classmates.

After everyone shared, I asked Elaine, in front of the whole class, if she wanted friends. She responded that she did. I then asked if anyone in the class would be willing to help Elaine to make and to be a better friend. Everyone, including Susan, raised their hands.

It is noteworthy to point out that when students feel a situation is addressed appropriately, and they have had a chance to be heard, they can be quite receptive to helping the perpetrator.

In addition to returning Susan's CD player, it was important that all of the students saw there is a natural consequence to the action of stealing. By law, if someone steals something, they go away for a while, usually to jail. In this case, Elaine was given the option of either being suspended for a day, (being away from her peers) or going into one of our younger grade classrooms and talking to the students about the importance of honesty and of not taking things that don't belong to you. Elaine chose to talk to the younger class.

This consequence allowed Elaine the opportunity to rectify her poor choice in some small way, by perhaps helping others not to make the same "mistake" she made. Furthermore, it sent the message to other students that we all have consequences for our behavior.

ENGAGING PEERS IN HELPING THE BULLY

Naturally when children are bullying they do not want to be discovered, and when they are found out, they tend deny it and attempt to bully in more subtle ways. However, if the school community is set up to educate students about bullying and to promote a "no tolerance" policy for bullying, then the majority of children are going to be vocally opposed to bullying.

In these circumstances students will talk to adults if they are being bullied and will talk about it with their peers as well. They also may point out children who are doing the bullying even if they themselves aren't victims.

In other words, the children learn that bullying is never acceptable and they share that "school wide" value with one another and the staff. The staff or other adult then has the opportunity to begin working with the bully.

Once an adult has made a connection with the bully and a relationship between an adult and the bully is formed, the bully will often be willing to accept the help offered. While exactly how the adult will help comes in many ways, one of the things the adult can do is ask the bully if he is willing to talk to his class about the issue of bullying, and to ask children's support with what might be called their "project." (This was offered in the previous example with Elaine.)

The bully may not initially feel safe enough to have this class discussion, however, depending on the classroom culture and degree of emotional/social safety, the bully may consider it at some point. If the bully does not wish to initiate this conversation with the adult's help, it will likely occur in some form anyway at her weekly class chat. (See part 3.)

TEACHER MODELING

Students learn the values of a school and classroom community, not by being told how they should behave, but by watching the communication and actions that occur in that environment on a daily basis. The tone of student's behavior is set by the modeling of the adults who are in charge of them.

It is nearly impossible (and also hypocritical) to elicit thoughtful, respectful actions and words between students when we, as educators, are not willing to utilize these actions ourselves. Here's an example illustrating this point:

The class was reading a book together and Tyra was clearly not following along. The teacher called on Tyra with a question and Tyra responded that she does not know the answer. The teacher has a choice to make at that point. Here are two possible responses:

> "Of course you can't answer the question, Tyra, because as usual, you are not paying attention. Perhaps if you paid attention to your work, your grades might improve."
>
> "Tyra, it looks like you lost your place. I'm wondering, Joey, if you can show Tyra what page we are on so that she can follow along and be ready to read in a few minutes when it's her turn."

In the first response, which unfortunately happens more than you might suspect, Tyra is embarrassed and humiliated in front of the whole class. While she should have been following along with the reading, the fact that she wasn't does not justify this response from the teacher.

In addition to Tyra feeling embarrassed, other students quickly understand that they will be spoken to in this way if they are not doing the right thing. While viewing that incident may help students follow along, in fear of being singled out as Tyra was, it also delivers a message to students that humiliating and embarrassing others is acceptable behavior in certain situations, when in fact, it is never acceptable.

The second response, conveyed respectfully, provides Tyra with the message she needs to hear, while also allowing her to adjust her actions and resume the reading activity with the rest of the class. More importantly, it provides a positive model of speaking to others, even when they are not in compliance with the activity.

Role modeling is more important than many educators and parents realize. Children really will do what you do instead of doing what you say they should do. If what you do and what you say they should do is congruent, you're giving them a great advantage.

DESIGNATE AN ADULT MENTOR

At our school, whenever we notice a child bullying others we discuss this in our faculty meetings. During the discussion we decide how each faculty member can reach out in some way to make a connection with the bully.

This may include engaging the bullying student in a conversation, asking the student to help out in some way, getting involved in a game or activity that student is playing at recess or lunch, and so on.

One teacher (usually the student's classroom teacher) is designated as the bullying student's mentor. That teacher agrees to connect with the student every day in a way that is separate from the daily classroom conversations and interactions.

In addition to engaging the student in any of the above-mentioned activities, the teacher may sustain an ongoing conversation with the student about the child's home life, personal interests, and other issues of importance to the student. The two of them may decide to engage in an ongoing project together (i.e., building a computer, working on a model airplane, playing the guitar).

The goal of this type of mentoring is to help the student learn and understand the value of healthy relationships, through connecting with the student on a humanistic level.

PROVIDING POSITIVE FEEDBACK

Bullies tend to have difficulty with regard to perspective-taking skills. Consequently, they often see situations only from their own point of view, and don't take into account anyone's feelings but their own.

As bullies are engaged in environments where children routinely discuss their thoughts and feelings, and the bully's own thoughts are elicited and responded to, the bully will begin to develop empathy for others.

At this point, the bully will begin to act and talk in ways that are respectful and helpful to others. Even if these actions are small, it is critical to acknowledge them. The following is an example:

Dominic was a fourth-grade bully who regularly teased a particular boy, Brent, who had special needs.

One day after the designated mentor had worked on this issue with Dominic for a period of time (with many setbacks), Dominic saw Brent crying on the play yard. He went up and asked Brent what was wrong. Brent explained that he hurt his leg, and Dominic brought him to the teacher.

The teacher took care of Brent and then went to find Dominic, saying, "Dominic, thank you so much for bringing Brent to me when he was injured. You know, I realize you have been working on behaving in a more friendly manner toward Brent. Today was a big step toward that goal. How did it make you feel to help Brent in that way?" Dominic admitted that it felt nice to be able to help Brent.

The feedback we give children helps solidify the positive feelings they personally gain from their thoughtful and friendly actions. It is important to remember not to judge those actions yourself by labeling them as right or good. It is more helpful to simply state what the actions were (friendly, thoughtful, caring, sensitive) and let the child react to how those actions made him feel.

Chapter Seven

Creating Opportunities for Bullies to Help Others

While it is important for all students to have the opportunity to help others, it is particularly critical for bullies to learn that they, as human beings, are valuable people who can positively impact the lives of others, and that they are also valuable members of your school community. Here is another example:

When Casey was bullying other students, in addition to being assisted by her fifth-grade teacher, she was invited into the kindergarten classroom during her lunch period to read a story to the class twice per week.

This not only got Casey off the yard periodically, giving herself and others a much-needed break, but Casey thoroughly enjoyed being able to read to the younger ones. As a result, the kindergarteners got to know Casey and each time she passed their classroom, many of them ran out to give her hugs. Casey immensely enjoyed this positive attention.

This positive attention was integral in Casey learning she didn't need to bully.

MEET WITH THE BULLY AND THE BULLY'S PARENTS

It's critical that the staff meet with both the bully and the parents of a bully at the same time. The parents need to know what's going on. Such a meeting, properly handled, can help enroll the parents in solving the problem. It must be made clear to all parties that the meeting is NOT punitive.

The goal of the meeting (which should be discussed with the child by a teacher or administrator before the meeting occurs) is to inform the parents about the issues their child is working on at school in regard to the child's behavior.

A further goal is to engage the child in this discussion so that the child can elicit support from the parents regarding how the parents can support the child with this at home.

It is important to discuss with the parents the progress their child has already made and your confidence that this progress will continue. These conversations often prompt parents to discuss relevant issues and parenting dilemmas that they are experiencing at home.

Many parents welcome advice and input with these issues if it is given in a nonjudgmental manner, without criticizing their actions. Because it's true that many children who bully are often bullied at home by parents or siblings, talking to the parents and engaging them in the process of helping their child can be extremely beneficial.

USE HUMOR AND HAVE FUN

Working with bullies is a serious and challenging endeavor. In undertaking this challenge, and working under the premise that bullies are not bad people but rather people who are hurting and upset, we can often reach bullies by connecting with them through humor and playful activities.

These activities serve to help us connect with students who are bullying others, while also engaging them with their peers in playful activities. The result is that students who are bullying others begin to see that they are capable of enjoying themselves and their peers in healthy and productive ways.

As an example, Perry came to our school in middle school and was not happy to be there. He liked his old school and felt that his parents made him change schools for arbitrary reasons. Perry was vocal about his dislike of our school and he bullied other kids immediately upon his arrival.

In addition to working with Perry, we invited him to join our Boys Club, an after-school activity where the older boys played tackle football on the field with teachers and administrators every Friday.

Initially, Perry refused to attend, even though he had to stay after school until his parents picked him up, but with persuasion, Perry decided to check it out. Fortunately, Perry thoroughly enjoyed Boys Club.

While some students (including the students he bullied) were a bit hesitant to play with Perry, we assured those boys that we would monitor the game closely.

Children who did not want to be tackled were permitted to opt for "two-handed touch" instead of being tackled and because adults played as well, it was a lot easier for them to actively monitor the play. It was a tradition to walk to a store for ice cream each week after the game.

Through Boys Club, and our walk to the store for ice cream each week after our game, Perry began to relate to other students in a more positive way. As he and other students got to know each another, Perry developed friendships with some of the children, and also developed feelings of safety and comfort with several of the teachers who participated. Boys Club served as a venue to reaching and connecting with Perry.

Other activities our teachers have used to add fun and humor to their day include:

- Bubblegum–blowing contests.
- Class walks around the neighborhood to collect random items for a class project.
- Spontaneous class challenges. (i.e., Who wants to join in a contest to try to eat five saltine crackers in one minute? Whoever can accomplish this task gets a homework pass for one night.) By the way, it is impossible to eat five saltine crackers in one minute without water!
- Taking time with the class to break open a baseball-size jawbreaker with a hammer and allowing the class to eat it.
- Class games of hide-and-seek.

Obviously, a major key to the success of these activities is adequate adult supervision and connection. Needless to say, these types of activities benefit all students, not only the children who bully others. Nonetheless, they have proven extremely beneficial in assisting children who bully to form connections and have fun with their peers in ways that are safe and mutually satisfying.

WHAT IS NOT HELPFUL/ HARMFUL IN WORKING WITH BULLIES

When working with bullies, in addition to understanding the tools and skills that are likely to be productive in our efforts, it's also helpful to understand those things that don't work.

The following are practices that we have found to be not only unhelpful, but potentially harmful in changing the bully's undesirable behavior:

- Physical punishment

Numerous studies have revealed that bullies are often victims of physical punishment and that it is highly likely that physical punishment contributes to their bullying behavior.

Physical punishment initiated by other students, parents, siblings, or any other person is not acceptable. If we expect our students to refrain from physically hurting other people, we must model that behavior in all areas of our lives as well.

It is a perplexing paradox to see a parent spanking their child and at the same time yelling, "I told you that it is not okay to hit people, including your brother." I often wonder if that parent is aware of the twisted message this action conveyed to their child. It is equally disturbing to hear educators belittle, humiliate, or embarrass students and then expect those same students to speak respectfully to one another.

- Hurtful verbal communication

Whether at home or at school, we tend to shame, embarrass, humiliate, and verbally attack the bully as a result of our anger and frustration at the bully for harming others.

When we act this way our goal is to make the bully see, feel, and comprehend how those actions have impacted another person. It doesn't work.

Often, our responses to bullying behavior are not only ineffective, but are forms of bullying as well. While the intent may be to help the bully develop awareness and empathy, responding to the bully in any of the above ways is more likely to inflict another hurt onto a person who is already hurting.

Furthermore, the bully may be more likely to disregard their own action if responded to in these ways, and instead, focus on your inappropriate response. By focusing on your inappropriate response, they avoid having to take responsibility for their actions.

- Isolating the bully

It is intriguing to witness many people's responses to a child who has misbehaved. Often it consists of some sort of isolation. Some of the more common responses include:

- Placing a child in a time out.
- Sending a child outside of the classroom (or at home, to her bedroom).
- Sitting a child down alone on a bench at recess.
- Refusing to talk to a child who has misbehaved.

All of these consequences of misbehavior are about isolating a child who was not behaving in a manner that is acceptable in the situation. The problem with isolating children is that when children are acting out in any way, they are really letting us know that they are upset and need our help.

Children who are not hurting, upset, and in need of attention will not seek attention by bullying. When we isolate a child for bullying or other negative behavior when they are hurting and upset, we cannot be there to help them, as the following example illustrates.

Keith was five years old and hit other children on the yard when he became frustrated and overwhelmed. After explaining to Keith that hitting was not acceptable and discussing other options he could use when he became frustrated, Keith's teacher allowed him to play on the yard with the other students.

On the occasions when Keith hit another child, his teacher would calmly let him know that this behavior was not okay and since he made an unacceptable choice, he lost his turn to play in the yard for the remainder of the play period and he would have to sit with the teacher.

While sitting, they would discuss the incident and the choice Keith had made to hit his peer. Then the teacher would remind Keith that he would be given another opportunity to play with kids at the next play period.

It is important to always give the child another chance to be successful in the environment. Keith would also have a teacher-mediated discussion with the peer he had hit before returning to play with the children.

There is a major difference between separating a child and isolating the child. Naturally, a child who harms other children must be removed from their presence. This removal is likely to be more effective in producing the appropriate behavioral expectation if it is done in a way that is thoughtful and respectful of the child, even if we are upset ourselves with the child's behavior.

UNNATURAL/INAPPROPRIATE CONSEQUENCES

Children who act out and bully others often struggle with recognizing, accepting, and adhering to appropriate social behavior. They may also feel the need to dominate, manipulate, and belittle others, somehow rationalizing their actions as a way of feeling justified in their behavioral choices.

It is critical to help these children to accurately view and understand their actions so that they can eventually choose to make different, healthier choices. When children are dealt inappropriate and unnatural consequences, they often lose the opportunity to learn the necessary information that will help them change this behavior.

An unnatural or inappropriate consequence is one that has no relevance to the child's action. For example, an unnatural and inappropriate consequence for a child getting into a physical fight with another child would be to assign the perpetrator trash duty, where the child must pick up a specific number of bags of trash during recess or lunch period.

What in the world does trash pick-up have to do with fighting?

This example comes directly from my own experience as a twenty-five-year-old intern, fulfilling my counseling hours at a local middle school. I was so excited to get to middle school and work with those kids. I knew they needed help and I was ready to help them.

On my very first morning, a boy was sent to the counselor I was shadowing because he started a physical fight with another student.

While I was all geared up to help discuss the fight with the student, the counselor quickly shoved five bags into the student's hand and told him to go pick up trash. This was one of many experiences that helped me realize that our kids were in big trouble—and I was going to have a challenge in attempting to help them.

One time I called a parent to inform her that the teacher saw that her daughter had written all over another child's desk in ink in an attempt to get the other child in trouble. The girl's parent asked me if she should come pick up her daughter to bring her home early.

"No" I replied. "I'm only calling to let you know that she will be staying at school until 5:00 p.m. today because she will be washing all of the desks in the school after school is out."

After school, the student and I discussed her actions and the consequence. I was not angry or hurtful toward her, nor did I pass judgment on the choice she made. Instead, I asked her how she felt about her choice and what she might do differently next time. Then she cleaned the desks and went home. I also asked her mom not to further punish her, as she had already fulfilled her responsibility for her action.

Had I suspended the student, made her write out behavior standards, asked her to apologize for her actions, benched her at lunch for a week, or ostracized her in some way, it is likely that she would simply be angry that she was caught and hate me for punishing her.

By delivering a natural consequence (if you write on desks, you clean desks) and talking to the student in a calm, nonjudgmental manner, she was allowed to accept responsibility, take an action to repair her poor choice, and she had nobody else to blame for the incident.

The next day it is important to get the students together who were involved in the incident, so that the victim is able to tell the other student how she felt and the student who acted out is able to hear and respond to the victim's thoughts and feelings.

While we do not suggest asking children to apologize to one another, because an apology is pointless and insincere when given under duress, at the end of the conversation, we often ask the perpetrator if there is anything that person wishes to say to the other child about the incident. Usually the child who was at fault chooses to apologize.

MAKING EXCUSES FOR THE BULLY'S BEHAVIOR

We often see parents make excuses for their child's behavior. Sometimes teachers make excuses too, mainly because they don't always see the behavior for what it really is or they believe they have implemented the necessary actions in their classroom to prevent bullying, so it could not possibly be occurring.

In order to be able to help a student who is bullying others, all the adults involved must agree that the student's behavior is unacceptable and it must cease. Parents who attempt to justify or excuse the behavior must be educated and informed about bullying and their support needs to be elicited to help their child.

When spoken to in a respectful manner, beginning with the positive feelings you have for their student and the faith you have in the school's ability to work with them to help their child, parents are often able to let down their guard and listen to the facts about what is happening with their child.

Teachers must be open to the idea that some kids may be bullying in their classroom, despite their efforts to discourage bullying, and they must respond to the issues at hand.

Part IV — The Connection Factor

In our fifteen-year work with children at our school, we found that children bully, tease, and hurt other children because they feel disconnected from other students, adults, and family members.

One of the most important elements in any human being's life is connection with another human being.

This intense need for connection begins the moment a baby is born. He communicates and connects with mom and other family members and relies on this connection with others for warm, positive feedback on a continual basis. This connection enables the child to grow, develop, learn, build intelligence, and function as a happy, cooperative member of society.

When a child (or adult) feels connected to another human being, she feels emotionally safe to be who she is and to share herself with others. She feels loved, and secure enough to let her guard down and to move freely in her environment without fear, trepidation, or worry that she will be physically or emotionally harmed.

This feeling of connection is a key component to helping attain success at school. In addition to ceasing bullying behavior, building connections with children at school enables children to think and learn better as well. We have seen the following results in children as we have built connections and developed safety in our school environment:

- They have the ability to think and reason well and be flexible in their cognitive thought process. They have an open mind. They can take in information, share information. They are open to the learning process.
- They can work well with others. They can share, work out problems in a thoughtful way, try new activities, socialize with others, and conquer challenges in the classroom and on the play yard.

- They can reason well, control their impulses, use good judgment, monitor their attention span, engage others, retain learned material, and develop new skills and abilities.
- When children feel connected and cared for at school, they like school. They want to come to school. They feel that they are important, valued members of the school community and that their presence makes a positive difference in the classroom and in the school community.
- They enjoy the opportunity to work together, help one another and share their ideas. As they are listened to and valued as contributing members of the school community, they take ownership and pride in their schoolwork and their relationships with peers and teachers.

In other words, it's the sense of connection that allows children to function normally and to learn and to grow into productive, well-adjusted adults.

Chapter Eight

Practicing What We Preach

Before we can guide our students through this process of connecting, being vulnerable with one another, sharing thoughts and feelings in a safe environment, and taking social, emotional, and cognitive risks, we, as educators, must be willing to do this work ourselves, and to learn to support one another in this process.

Just as students do not walk through the doors as simply cognitive beings, effective teachers do not show up on a daily basis merely to teach lessons. Educators who hope to reach children and to make a difference in their lives must be willing to share more than their cognitive minds with their students. And they must be able to constantly look within themselves with an honest and open mind.

This kind of self-examination and self-knowledge is not for everyone! I have had several teachers walk right out of my school mid-interview (and unfortunately a couple even mid-school day) when they realized the commitment involved in creating a cognitively, emotionally, and socially safe school environment.

On the other hand, teachers in general typically enter this profession with the goal, hope, and desire to positively make a difference in the lives of students. They want to make connections with children and they need the support of their school administration to encourage them to do so.

The many teachers/staff who were able to connect with children in this way at our school found great fulfillment, not only professionally for the work they have been able to accomplish with children, but personally, due to the inner growth, strength, and rewards they have attained through the process of learning to listen, look within, risk, and work to develop connections with students and with one another.

HOW DO WE ADULTS GET CONNECTED?

Every year before school began, I spent two weeks with my faculty and staff. Those two-week periods were a time we were involved in training with regard to curriculum planning, policies, procedures, and other school-related issues that needed to be addressed.

However, in addition to accomplishing school business, we took ample time to engage in a variety of connecting activities as well.

These activities not only helped us bond as a faculty and staff, but they also provided teachers with ideas for activities that they could do with students in their classrooms. The teachers were able to witness, through firsthand experience, the process of participating in the experience that they would be asking their students to embark upon.

In addition to this two-week training period, our faculty/staff met for a two-and-a-half- to three-hour weekly meeting throughout the school year. We used part of this meeting time to discuss school business, student issues, and so on and part of the meeting time to focus on supporting one another.

The following are some activities that any faculty/staff may start with if they have not yet incorporated any bonding or connecting experiences into their training/meeting times:

- *Play Games.* Begin each meeting with an introductory game or activity that will help you get to know one another better and/or games and activities that give people the opportunity to work together on teams of three to five people to accomplish a given task.

There are many websites and books that offer examples of these types of games/activities. Some of these activities can take a few minutes and others require much more time. It is beneficial to invest the time in some of the more lengthy activities on a regular basis as they provide a tremendous amount of cohesiveness amongst the faculty/staff.

- *The BIG Outing.* Once each year, at the beginning of the year when we did our two-week training, I took the faculty/staff on a mandatory surprise outing. I'd tell them what time they must show up at school, what time they would return to school, and what clothing they should wear. Other than that, no information was given.

These outings were always physically challenging in some way, and required people to support one another. As people were at various stages of fitness, health, and range in ages, the outings could be quite intense.

Although we experienced a little blood (minor scrapes), and a lot of sweat and tears on our outings, they were the most productive and bonding experiences we embarked upon as a group.

I highly recommend that all faculty/staff groups take the time to experience a one-day outing together at the beginning of each year. Some groups take a one- or two-day retreat together, which is also fun and relaxing.

I definitely suggest spending time having dinners together and relaxing as a faculty/staff. However, the big, one-day outings were different in that they demanded that each participant challenge him/herself and support others who are also being challenged.

If the school you work at does not have the time or money to accommodate your group, then do it on a weekend and have each person put in a little money to cover the cost. It is worth it. The outing must be physically challenging AND there must be guides there to support the group to work together to overcome the challenges. Examples of some of the outings we have experienced included:

- Horseback dinner ride through the mountains.
- Hiking/ropes course.
- Zip lining and lunch outing.
- Challenging bike ride up a ski-lift and down the rugged mountains.
- Sailing trip where we sailed the boat.

In the process of venturing out to conquer our outings together, our faculty/staff had to encounter many obstacles and decide as a group how to move forward with our activity in light of these challenges.

When we went sailing, for example, one of our employees announced that she was deathly afraid of the ocean. When she found out (on the day of the trip) that we would be sailing on the ocean, she absolutely refused to participate. We all had to work together to figure out what to do about this problem and how to solve it in a way that worked for all of us.

Since I had already paid for the sailboat and guides for the day, this was a very tricky dilemma! In the end, some of us went sailing while others remained on the beach with the teacher who wouldn't sail. Afterward we all went out to eat together as a group.

Our bike-riding endeavor up the mountain to the ski lift and then down a treacherous mountain path was probably the most physically challenging group experience, and the scariest. We had to work through many challenges together in order to make it through that day.

Many people felt they could not physically do it. One teacher overcame her fear of bike riding that day, which was a remarkable reward. Others realized they were stronger and braver than they thought!

Zip lining was a challenge for our folks who were afraid of heights (myself included) and I really wasn't sure how well that trip was going to go. It ended up being helpful that I was terrified, and still willing to do it anyway, or at least try.

We had an amazing experience on five different zip lines that day. People supported one another to work through their fears and to embrace new challenges. Some who felt uncomfortable trying it were supported to do what they felt was right for themselves, as it is very important to challenge people but not push them beyond their limits.

Being fearful of heights, the zip-lining excursion was not something that was easy for me. In fact, I was quite nervous and I discussed my feelings with the teachers. We discussed how they could support me (and others who were also fearful). This discussion was helpful for all of us.

I realized that if I went first or second on each zip line, I wasn't so nervous about watching everyone else go before me while I stood nervously anticipating how scared I was going to be.

Of course it also helped knowing that I had no choice but to go forward with each zip line because the five lines went in a circle. Once you went on the first line, there was no way of getting back unless you completed the remainder of the lines.

All of these activities, in addition to bringing us closer as a group and being incredibly fun, helped teach our faculty/staff some important lessons about supporting children in the classroom to address and to overcome academic and non-academic issues that they face on a daily basis.

The day after each activity we take time to reflect upon the activity, discussing the following topics:

- What were your thoughts/feelings about the outing?
- What is something you learned about yourself?
- What is something you learned about the group?
- What are some things you learned that you think are applicable to your students?

Of course, there were no right or wrong answers to these questions. The sharing, however, helped us bond even more. Later, during the school year, we were able to draw on these experiences when we faced problem situations.

LISTENING TIME

Another important component of developing safety and connection amongst the faculty and staff is learning to really listen to one another. When one person talks about whatever is on his mind and other people listen without comments, judgment, or feedback, this can help the one being listened to off-load and process some of his thoughts and feelings in a safe environment.

Sometimes after a long day of working with students, before beginning a faculty meeting at the end of the day, pairing up for listening time can be helpful. Partners go to a private part of the room (or to separate rooms) and each one takes a three- to five-minute turn of talking while the other just listens.

The roles are then reversed.

The instructions are that when it is your turn to talk, you can talk about anything you want that is on your mind at the moment. It could be something that happened during the day, something you are upset about, something personal, something you are excited about, and so on.

The listener's job is to merely listen attentively, making eye contact, and providing an empathetic ear. No advice, comments, or interruptions are to be given by the listener. What is said in the listening partnership remains confidential within the listening partnership and is not to be repeated to anyone without the permission of your partner.

Once the group has developed closeness and safety, listening time can be implemented as a group process as necessary and will be welcomed by the group. For example, we experienced many occasions where someone at a faculty meeting was extremely upset about a personal or professional matter and asked if the group would be willing to listen.

In these instances we usually set aside ten to fifteen minutes to listen to that person.

After the talking was finished, and it was often accompanied by tears, we'd ask if the person would like feedback. If so, we spent some additional time providing feedback and then continued with our meeting. Often just the sharing was enough and the person didn't want feedback, so we moved on.

CHECK-IN

Beginning all faculty meetings with a brief "check-in" can be very beneficial in establishing group closeness. Faculty members take two or three minutes each to talk about how they are feeling and/or anything that is occurring in their personal or professional lives that they wish to share. It is sometimes easier to create a check-in topic for people, especially when you first start the process, because it helps people to find something to talk about.

Examples of check-in topics include:

- Talk about a highlight of your weekend.
- Talk about something that is going well in your life personally or professionally.
- Talk about a recent success you have had with regard to curriculum.
- Talk about a recent success you have had with regard to a relationship with a student.
- What would you say is your greatest strength as an educator?
- What is your greatest challenge as an educator?
- Talk about something you remember enjoying about a particular teacher you had during your elementary-school experience.
- What was something you disliked about school as a child? Why?

Checking in helps everyone to be grounded in what their job is. They become more present. It helps people let go of distractions and it helps build solid lines of communication.

Chapter Nine

Developing a School Anti-bullying Policy

One of the many benefits of incorporating physical, emotional, and social safety into your school's daily curriculum and operating procedures is that it becomes inherent that children and adults treat one another with respect and compassion.

It may seem unnecessary to develop an antibullying policy in schools where their foundation is built upon the commitment of creating safety. Nonetheless, antibullying policies, in addition to being required by many educational jurisdictions worldwide, send a vital message to the school community about the school's commitment to prevent bullying.

Adults, like children, are more invested in implementing policies and procedures when they are able to provide input into creating those policies. Hence, it is critical to solicit input from faculty, staff, and the students in developing a school antibullying policy.

The following are general guidelines that should be included in antibullying policies. As noted above, the specific details may vary a bit based on input of individuals. However, it is critical to include each component:

- A clear statement of the school's stance against bullying and the expectation that all members of the school community are responsible for treating people with civility and respect.
- A clear, concise definition of bullying, including a description of all forms of bullying.
- A detailed description of the policy, including the responsibilities and expectations of faculty/staff, administration, and students in regard to upholding the antibullying policy.

- A description of the actions that will be implemented at school to prevent bullying (for example, faculty/staff training, student awareness, curriculum content).
- An explanation of the responsibilities of school community members who witness bullying (parents, faculty/staff, other students).
- An action plan that will be implemented if cases of bullying occur or complaints of bullying are reported.
- A time frame for how often the policy will be reviewed, updated, and distributed to all members of the school community.

Inviting parents to attend school community meetings in order to inform them of the school's antibullying policy and to discuss the policy with them can be beneficial in increasing parent awareness. It can also open up a critical dialogue between parents and administrators, allowing parents to ask questions and gain insight into any bullying that may be occurring in their children's school.

In addition to discussions with parents, bullying education can be conveyed through guest speakers who are bullying experts, role-play scenarios, dialogue between parents and the faculty, or presentations of recommended books, movies, or articles on the various aspects and forms of bullying.

Part V — Bullying Prevention in the Classroom

Chapter Ten

This Is the Curriculum

One of the things educators often ask when they begin to learn about the commitment involved in building and sustaining safe learning environments for all children and teaching how to reduce and even eliminate bullying is, "When will we have time to fit it into the curriculum?"

My answer to that is always the same: "You can't have a curriculum without this!"

While our children are depressed, hurting one another, and committing suicide in our schools, educators (and the public and politicians) have yet to realize that we are wasting our time and money when we focus on test scores, Blue Ribbon Schools, and standardized education.

High test scores, if possible in an environment where bullying is the norm, mean we're leaving out a significant percentage of our students, those who bully and those who are bullied. A Blue Ribbon School that hasn't stopped bullying is only fulfilling part of its charge, and maybe the least important part.

So-called standardized education is an oxymoron that fosters bullying or at least depression.

Children live and breathe socially. If we are going to teach children well, we must be able to reach them on all levels, socially, emotionally, and cognitively. In order to do this, we must engage with students on a human level.

If we are able to develop meaningful relationships with children, show them that we care about them, that we are here to help them, to provide emotionally and socially safe learning environments, to listen to them, support and encourage them, and help them learn and grow with our caring guidance, only then do we have a chance of truly educating children.

When children feel safe and connected at school, we will not have to beat our heads against the wall trying to figure out how to get them to share in the responsibility of ensuring they are well educated. Children naturally want to learn and succeed in school. They are simply unable to do so if their attention is being diverted by having to protect themselves against a bully.

Even if they aren't being bullied themselves, children see others being bullied and they become fearful and preoccupied with trying to ensure they don't become the bully's next target.

If everyone isn't safe in school, no one can learn (or teach) well.

ESTABLISHING SAFE LEARNING ENVIRONMENTS

Regardless of a child's age, in order for him to be able to learn, he must feel physically and emotionally safe at school. He must feel valued, and heard. He must know that his thoughts and words are important and that he can share them without being criticized, judged, or ridiculed. He must feel connected to his peers and teachers and be able to communicate openly and effectively with them.

This type of communication promotes safety in the classroom and school community, paving the way for a more productive cognitive learning experience. As a result, the first order of business is to establish emotional safety by setting the groundwork in the classroom for a respectful and safe environment for all.

STUDENT-GENERATED CLASSROOM RULES

While there is always a need for teacher-generated rules, it is productive to involve the class in a discussion about their expectations in regard to behavior and classroom rules. You will find that children will be much more invested in upholding the rules if they are included in the process of making them.

Children are also more creative about the rules they come up with than teachers are. Additionally, allowing children the opportunity to establish some of the rules helps the teacher to understand some of the real issues that the kids are concerned about.

In one particular classroom a second-grade child raised her hand during our rules discussion and said that she didn't think kids in the class should be allowed to "disclude" other kids who want to play with them.

This led to a great discussion about how children feel when other children don't want to play with them and led to a rule in the class that everyone is allowed to play in everyone else's games at snack and lunch.

TEACHER MODELING

It is critical that teachers speak respectfully to students at all times. If we expect children to express their feelings without yelling, blaming, criticizing, or accusing others then we, as teachers, must be able to do the same with them.

The relationship between teachers and students is a critical one. If a child feels respected and valued by a teacher, that teacher will be able to teach her anything. However, if that trust and respect is not established, or it gets broken, it will be difficult to reach and therefore teach the student.

The key to establishing that trust is through connecting with the student by listening to her and really knowing her, by letting her know that you value her as a person and genuinely care about what she has to say. Your ability as a teacher to connect with students sets the stage for emotional safety in the classroom, and determines your effectiveness in teaching the academic curriculum as well.

SPECIAL TIME AT SCHOOL

Another great way to create a safe learning environment and develop connections with children is by spending special time with them. Special time consists of spending one-on-one time with a child where the teacher is giving the child undivided attention by participating in a conversation, game, or activity chosen by the child. In a school environment, special time activities may include:

- Having a little picnic lunch with a student.
- Playing a card game or board games during snack.
- Meeting for a private chat before, during, or after school.
- Playing guitar or other musical instrument together during snack or lunch.
- Building a model airplane or car together (or other project) over a period of time at planned free break periods.

Special time does not have to last for long periods of time and often occurs in ten- to fifteen-minute increments.

Sometimes special time activities consist of a teacher spending time with two children together. This may occur if a teacher (or a child) notices that two children seem to have a particularly difficult time getting along with one another and are, for example, continually getting into arguments and disagreements.

The teacher will invite the two children to do something special together with the teacher and will use that activity to attempt to help the two children strengthen their association.

On one occasion, two third-grade boys in the same class were experiencing difficulties in their relationship. They often argued over seemingly inconsequential matters, picked on each other, and constantly set each other off.

A teacher decided to walk them down the street to the market and allow them to pick out a treat to surprise the class with at the end of the day.

On the way to the store, the teacher asked them a variety of questions about themselves to help them get to know each other a little better. She asked simple things like: what's your favorite movie? video game? sport? food? color? subject in school? television show?

When they arrived at the market, they had to decide together what snack to select for the class. By the time they finished and arrived back at school, the boys knew more about one another, realized they had more in common than they previously had thought, and were warmly greeted by a class full of kids who were happy to receive an unexpected treat.

Of course this did not solve all of the boys' issues with one another, but it served as an opportunity to shift their relationship from a negative place to a more hopeful one.

FACILITATION OF CLASSROOM PROBLEM-SOLVING ISSUES

Teachers help students learn effective communication and problem-solving skills by facilitating problem-solving discussions with the children. When teachers solve all of the problems for children and step in to help by judging and condemning a child for his behavior, the child is often left feeling guilty and found out. There's no opportunity for the offender to acknowledge and own his actions in any given situation.

On the other hand, when adults can step back and moderate in a nonjudgmental way, they empower children to understand and take responsibility for themselves and their actions. This works best when it is done in a natural way.

Generally, the best approach is with a simple conversation. As children are exposed to these conversations on a daily basis, they internalize this type of dialogue and it becomes natural to them. The goal is for children to be able to solve problems with peers on their own, without teacher intervention.

The following are some everyday examples of how to help children develop communication skills and work on student centered problem solving:

- A child Joe is speaking angrily to another child Andy.

Rather than the teacher telling Joe not to talk to Andy like that, the teacher walks over and says, "Joe I hear you talking to Andy in a very loud voice. You sound upset. Can I help you talk to Andy in a voice that might be a little easier for him to listen to, or would you like to talk to him a little later when you are not feeling so angry?"

This gives Joe two choices and also lets Andy know he's being protected.

- Two children are arguing and pulling on a toy.

When the teacher comes over, instead of taking the toy and saying that neither child can have it, the teacher says, "Wow, I see you are both upset and really want that toy. I'm going to take the toy for a moment so we can talk about a plan for how to share the toy."

The teacher takes the toy and gives each child a turn to discuss his idea for sharing the toy. The teacher may have a better idea about how the sharing could work, but does not share her idea. She lets kids work out a plan, giving a little input here and there.

It's surprising how well this approach can work, with a little bit of effort on the teacher's part. Here's an example:

One time our kindergarten kids were upset because we only had three swings on the playground. As you might imagine, the three kids who got there first never wanted to give up their seat which meant they were the only kids who got to swing on them during the twenty-minute snack break.

After snack the class had a discussion about how only three children getting to swing was unfair. They came up with a decision that each kid could only be on the swing for a ten-minute turn.

Children at this age have little sense of time and the teachers knew how that was going to play out—only two groups of three kids would get on the swings. But the teachers didn't tell the kids because they knew that the kids needed to figure it out. Not only that, the whole group agreed with the plan and all the children were excited because they were united in a new agreement.

After a few days, the kids worked their way down to two- and three-minute turns on the swings if someone else was waiting for a turn. It was a tremendously productive learning experience for them on many levels.

In an older classroom two kids were upset because one girl, Jane, said something about another girl, Sally. Sally began to cry.

The teacher, instead of sending Jane to the office, said to Jane, "Sally looks really upset, let's see what's going on." The teacher then listened to Sally who told the teacher that Jane called her a "big butt" and the other kids laughed. Jane immediately said that she was only joking and didn't mean it.

The teacher responded with, "Jane, I want you to look at Sally's face. Do you think it was funny to Sally?" Jane reluctantly admitted that, no, it probably wasn't funny to Sally.

Next, the teacher said, "Sally, what would you like to say to Jane about this?" Sally responded telling Jane she hadn't thought it was funny at all. Then the teacher asked Jane if there is anything she wants to say to Sally about it.

It is not recommended that teachers insist or even suggest that children apologize for their behavior.

In this case, our experience is that Jane will undoubtedly apologize before too long. Children who are supported well and who are not shamed, criticized, and made to feel guilty will naturally feel badly for hurting another person and will apologize on their own.

Chapter Eleven

Class Chats: What's Going Well? What's Not?

There are so many benefits to having a weekly chat in the classroom. The purpose of the chats is to discuss the things that are going well and the things that are not going well in the class.

CHAT GUIDELINES

The following Chat Guidelines, which should be established before the first chat, help set the behavioral expectations for the chat:

- One person speaks at a time.
- Each person listens thoughtfully and with an open mind when someone is speaking.
- When it's your turn to speak, state your own thoughts, feelings, and opinions in a respectful manner.
- Do not comment negatively on someone else's thoughts, feelings, and opinions.
- Do not give people advice.
- Be respectful of opinions that are different from your own.

Always begin the discussion with things that are going well in the class. These things may be academic, social, or anything the kids state they feel is going well in the class. Asking kids to begin with the good things helps them learn to focus on the positive, even in the midst of problems.

Sometimes when children (or adults) are upset and burdened with a problem, it is difficult for them to see past their upsets to any other positive things happening in their lives. Beginning with good things helps children remember that there actually are some good things happening with and around them!

After we've talked about the good things, we move to the problems happening in the class. A child who wishes to share a problem must also have shared something that is going well, even if the good thing is something small.

Children share various types of problems during these chats. Problems range from the fact that they feel they get too much work and not enough play time, and so on to social issues such as, "Jan is unfriendly to some of the girls and only wants certain girls to sit with her at lunch," or "Bill wants to have a Baseball Card Club but doesn't want Jim to join the club." Still other issues are more personal and must be handled very carefully.

Once, in a third-grade class I taught, there was a boy, Charles, who constantly farted in class loudly and obviously. The children were very annoyed and disgusted by this and another boy, Eric, who sat next to Charles, brought it up at chat.

Following our guidelines, Eric very kindly said, "Charles, I really don't like it when you fart loudly and then laugh because it is kind of gross and it makes me not want to sit by you. So I was wondering if you could please stop."

At first Charles gave excuses as to why he farted so often claiming to have stomach problems. However, after some mediation, and an arrangement where Charles could step outside when he felt it necessary, he agreed to try to work toward stopping this behavior.

Something wonderful that happens as a result of this type of discussion; it paves the way for us to talk about the fact that we are all working on things in our lives. Children are then able to recognize they are not alone with problems and talk about things that they are working on.

Once these issues are identified, the teachers and children can talk about issues when they arise in a nonpunitive way, often saying something like, "Hey guys, remember Jake is working on waiting for his turn and it's feeling really hard for him to wait right now. Maybe we can help him." Or, "Tina is working on what it means to be a friend. I'm wondering if we can help her figure out her problem with Jill right now."

Helping everyone remember what someone is working on sometimes helps lessen the feelings that come up in other children around a child's challenging behavior and it can help children deal with their peers empathetically rather than angrily.

Another great benefit of classroom chats is that they can help diffuse bullying very quickly.

One year we had a fifth-grade student, Regina, who was being unfriendly to several other girls in the class. Many girls were afraid to say that Regina was acting mean because they didn't want to make the situation worse with Regina, or to have Regina turn on them.

One day in a chat a girl, Rachelle, finally shared what Regina was doing. This opened the door for other girls to share their stories about Regina. The class talked to Regina about her behavior and how it affected them. They discussed why Regina acted this way and asked her to stop treating people badly. The girls agreed to check in at the next chat to see how things were progressing.

It is critical when problems are brought up in chat that teachers remember to check in at the next chat about what's happening with that problem.

In this case, Regina was absent for the next chat. In fact, over the next two months, the teacher noticed that Regina was often absent on chat days and she realized that it was because Regina did not want to face her peers in a chat session.

The teacher called home and explained the situation to Regina's mom and asked the mother to make sure that Regina was healthy on chat days. From then on, Regina began to have no choice but to be accountable for her behavior and we were able to work with Regina on this issue to help her start treating her peers better.

IN THE CAN CHATS

Sometimes children do not want to say problems they are thinking about out loud in the class chat. A helpful idea is to keep a can or box in the classroom where children can anonymously drop handwritten problems that need to be stated but that children may feel are too scary to state aloud.

The teacher reads those problems aloud during the "not going well" section of the chat. Examples of such problems from third-, fourth-, and fifth-grade classes include:

- "Mark says bad words like the "f" word when the teachers aren't around."
- "Alice and Courtney won't let other kids in their Coolest Girls Club."
- "I feel like I don't have a lot of friends in this class."
- "I am sick of Brody wasting all of our time by interrupting the kids and teachers."
- "Math is getting boring. We haven't had a game day in three weeks."
- "I don't like sitting by Jenny because she smells badly."

Each is an example of the kind of things kids don't want to say out loud in front of the whole class. It's worth noting that in each example, the children were able to chat their way to a solution, not only solving the problem and learning to be real problem solvers, but reducing the bullying to almost nothing.

OLDER KIDS CHAT

Middle-school and high-school chats are formatted a bit differently than elementary-school chats and serve a different purpose.

While the goal of chats in elementary school is to help children learn effective communication and problem-solving skills as well as developing a safe and connected classroom environment, chats at the older level provide students the opportunity to discuss and explore their thoughts, feelings, and opinions on topics that are interesting and important to them in a safe environment without judgment and criticism.

Here, children choose a topic and the kids and adults discuss some aspect of that topic. The chat is confidential, meaning that what is said in the chat, stays in the chat. Children are told before the chat begins what types of things that adults (teachers) are not allowed to keep confidential so that the children understand what kinds of issues teachers must report if they should arise in chat. Other than that, teachers agree to confidentiality.

It is critical to inform parents about these type of chats and to let them know about the confidentiality guidelines before having the first chat with children. Confidentiality can be difficult for some families to accept, as children will often discuss their drug and alcohol use or sexual experience during a chat.

Not surprisingly, parents feel they should be privy to these disclosures. Informing parents of the reasons for the confidentiality can often help them understand both the value of the chats and the need for confidentiality.

As educators, we are there to support children and help them to explore their actions and behaviors, examine why they may or may not choose to participate in a particular behavior, and help children determine what factors are involved in making good, healthy decisions for themselves. Teachers are not there to tell children what is right or wrong.

Even when teachers try to set morality rules, we find children don't usually listen to what we tell them to do. However, children do tend to respect adults who listen to their thought process; ask respectful, thought-provoking questions; and trust them enough to support them to make their own decisions.

Typical topics of discussion for middle-school and high-school chats include:

- Drugs/alcohol
- Sex
- Relationships
- Gender issues
- Family issues
- Politics

Middle-school and high-school students are often reluctant to initiate a conversation around topics like these; choosing from a list makes it easier. They may choose the topic they wish to discuss, such as "relationships in our class," but will then ask for help to move the conversation forward.

The main difference between these students and elementary students is older students don't necessarily wish to discuss specific issues with one another because they have learned to address these issues on their own. They are more interested in talking about deeper relationship issues.

Before the chat begins, students are informed of the topic and are given the choice to remain in the chat or leave if they do not wish to participate. Remaining means they are agreeing to participate, both as a speaker and as a listener.

We begin by passing around a can containing questions written about the topic on individual pieces of paper. The questions are to be created by a teacher, counselor, or administrator who knows the dynamics of the particular group of students. Each child chooses a question as the can comes around, reads it aloud, and answers it.

The following are some questions that children have answered during chat on the topic of "relationships in our class":

- Name three people in here that you do not feel close to. Why are you not close to them? What could you do to be closer?
- Who is someone in this room that you respect and admire? Why do you respect this person? In what ways are you similar to this person? In what ways do you want to be more like this person?
- In what ways would you change this class if you could, both socially and/or academically?
- If you had to spend one week alone with someone in this room for the purpose of getting to know that person better and just hanging out together, who would you choose? Why?
- How do you feel that you have changed personally this year? How would you like to change even more? How will you accomplish this? How can we help you with this?

- If you are the type of person who has a difficult time sharing and opening up in class, if you rarely offer your thoughts, feelings, and opinions, tell us why that is.
- If this does NOT apply to you, hand this to someone that you feel it DOES apply to and you can pick another question after that person answers this question.
- How do you think this class has changed so far this year? How would you like to see it change even more in the next month or two? Do you feel connected to the kids in here? Why or why not?
- Who is someone in this room that you feel you know hardly anything about? Why haven't you gotten to know this person? What would you want to ask this person if you could ask three questions? Do it now!
- Who is someone in here that you would like to have a closer relationship with? Why don't you have that relationship with that person? What will you do to change that? What would you like to ask of that person in regard to your relationship with him or her?

Each of these questions sets the stage and provides material for the remainder of the chat discussion.

Another thing to do with the older kids chat is to have the children choose a topic of discussion and then allow them to put comments or questions in the can that are focused on that topic.

The agreement is that any question can be asked and will be answered honestly. The questions are usually answered by the adults in the chat as well, unless a question is directed to the children. Children are welcome to add their thoughts and comments to our answers.

Teachers do not provide personal information about their lives. (Once during a sex topic, one of the questions asked of a male teacher was in regard to the number of times he had intercourse with his wife each week. That question was not allowed.)

Each person can put several questions or comments in the can. The children especially enjoy this type of chat when it comes to certain topics such as sex and/or drugs and alcohol, because this venue provides them the anonymity to ask questions that they are quite curious about but are afraid to ask in front of their peers.

Here are some examples of questions we have been asked in middle-school chats:

- How do lesbians have sex?
- Why do condoms come in different flavors?
- Has anyone in here ever had feelings about, thought they might be, or know they are gay?
- If you try drugs once can you get addicted?

- Raise your hand if you have ever been drunk. (When kids raise their hands, we go around and ask kids whose hands are raised if they are willing to share anything about this experience with the group.)

Chats can also be utilized with specific groups of children. Having an "all sixth-grade boys chat" at lunch for example, where the guys all bring their lunches and the teacher perhaps provides a popsicle treat for dessert, can be a nice experience. The boys can talk about the things that are going well and any challenges in their relationships, or any activities they are looking forward to, either individually or as a group.

One year we had a bunch of fourth-grade girls who always wanted to have a lunch chat. They really had no problems, but loved to get together in my office to talk. During the chats they planned a dance for all of the fourth graders, which turned out to be quite fun!

The older girls often like to have a lunch chat to discuss their boy dilemmas and who-likes-who, whereas the boys, often less socially mature than the girls, like to talk about video games, computers, and various other gadgets.

Part VI — Bullying Prevention in the Larger School Community

Chapter Twelve

Appreciating and Enjoying One Another

The power of appreciating another human being is an amazing thing. Appreciation circles support the development of safety and connectedness in the classroom by helping everyone understand their value to one another and to the class as a whole.

Appreciation circles usually take place on a person's birthday (or thereabouts if the birthday falls on a nonschool day). Everyone sits in a circle and each person takes a turn saying something appreciative about the person whose birthday it is. The appreciation cannot be a physical trait or characteristic. Rather, it has to be about a quality the person has, like kindness or thoughtfulness or humorousness, and so on.

When doing a birthday appreciation circle, we usually ask the person whose birthday it is to give an appreciation about him or herself as well.

Appreciation circles can also happen randomly on any given day. The class can sit in a circle and the teachers says, "Today we are going to go around the circle and each of you will say something you appreciate about the person sitting next to you on the right side." This way, each person is able to give and receive an appreciation.

In the younger grades, children often have difficulty thinking of a quality that they respect about a person. Often they may state something they like or appreciate doing or playing with that person.

Examples of kindergarten to second-grade appreciations include:

- I appreciate that you play the wagon game with me.
- I appreciate that you sit by me at lunch.
- I appreciate doing block buildings with you because you listen to my ideas.

- I appreciate that you help me when I am sad.

As children get older the appreciations become more personal and detailed. Examples of third- to sixth-grade appreciations include:

- I appreciate that you are funny, thoughtful, and a good friend to me.
- I appreciate that we have fun together and that you're easy to talk to.
- Jane, you are my best friend and I appreciate that you always listen to me.
- I appreciate that you are honest, trustworthy, and you like to play with me.

By the time children are in middle school, they are able to put together several sentences to describe their appreciation for a peer.

In conducting appreciation circles over the past fifteen years, we have observed the following interesting behavior in children:

- It is often difficult for children, especially children who have not sat through an appreciation circle before, to sit in a circle and listen to appreciations from their peers. In fact, some kids are so uncomfortable hearing people say nice things to them, that they literally get up and start moving around the room, talking, and distracting the kids who are trying to appreciate them.
- Children who feel badly about themselves have a very difficult time finding anything at all to appreciate about another person. We insist at the appreciation circles that all children say something they appreciate or something they like to do with the person whose birthday it is. On many occasions it has taken a very long time for certain children to think of anything to say to a peer, even if they are great friends with that person. It seems to be the children with the lowest self-esteem who have the most difficulty with this.
- Everyone has a difficult time saying something they appreciate about themselves. All kids seem to squirm a bit when asked to think about a quality in themselves that they appreciate and then state it aloud in front of their peers.
- Regardless of their age, all the kids are more excited about and look forward to their appreciation circle, more than they do to their cake, ice cream, or whatever other treat they have for their birthday celebration, confirming the fact that children really do care. They want to be valued, appreciated, and to know that their presence makes a positive difference in the lives of others.

HAVING FUN AS A SCHOOL COMMUNITY

Part of establishing safe learning environments is creating both structured and unstructured opportunities for children in the school of all ages to interact with one another. As younger children become familiar with older students, the older students seem to become more human and less scary.

Older students begin to soften toward the little ones as these older kids play and become reacquainted with the young, playful side of themselves and enjoy activities that they've long since forgotten were enjoyable, such as swinging on swings, playing with blocks, and jumping rope.

Some structured, all-school activities that can be quite successful in bringing students together as a school community are:

- *All-School Lunch.* Once each month, the whole school eats lunch together in a designated location like the auditorium, courtyard, or grassy field. One class is responsible for preparing and serving the lunch to the rest of the school community. The lunch can take place toward the end of the week so that the class preparing the lunch, with the teacher's help, can decide at the beginning of the week what the menu will be.

The kids responsible for the lunch go around and tell everyone what they will be serving. They also tell children to bring a designated amount of money to help pay for the food, generally between $2 and $5 each.

A few parents usually help the class prepare the food on all-school lunch day and the class serves all the students and teachers in the school. Students of all ages sit together. Nobody is allowed to sit alone at all-school lunch; teachers and administrators eat with the kids too!

- *All-School Assemblies.* Every month the whole school gets together for an assembly. The assembly is run by the class that has been assigned to run assemblies as their school job; usually sixth graders are a good age group to run assemblies.

The designated class sets up for the assembly, informs the other classrooms when and where the assembly will be, and prepares discussion topics and activities for the assembly. Two children from the class run the assembly.

They often begin by asking children to raise their hands if they wish to comment on anything that is going well for them or that they are enjoying in school. After that, the assembly leaders ask if children would like to discuss any problems that are happening or things that are not going well in the school community.

The leaders explain that this is not a time to share classroom issues as students can do that in their classroom chats.

The following are examples of common school issues children have shared in all-school assembly:

- The bathrooms are stinky because kids don't flush the toilet.
- We don't have enough toys to play with in the yard.
- We don't like the hot lunch program because the food tastes bad.
- Kids leave their trash on the lunch tables at snack and lunch.

Although it is clearly stated that this is a venue for school issues, sometimes children will bring up problems they are having at home during the all-school assembly. Regardless of the problem, the assembly leaders (with assistance from a teacher as needed) solicit solutions from children and facilitate a discussion about the possible solutions.

It is helpful to write a list of the problems on a white board at the beginning of the discussion and then decide which one or two problems to discuss during the assembly. Spending too much time discussing problems can be frustrating, and difficult for the leaders to keep the attention of those students who are not invested in the given problem.

After the problems are discussed, ending the assembly with a fun activity is always recommended as a way to connect the whole school community through playfulness, laughter, and just plain fun! Here are some great all-school fun activities:

- *Teacher Impersonations.* The assembly leaders explain that children are able to come up and do an impersonation of any teacher. They explain that the impersonation should not be mean-spirited or vindictive, but should be funny or fun.

The other children watch and then try to guess who the kids are impersonating. Before they begin, the leaders always ask if there are any teachers or administrators that do not wish to be impersonated.

Children are also not permitted to impersonate a teacher or administrator who is not present in the assembly. This is important because it helps children to understand that having fun in this way is acceptable if it is done in a thoughtful way with mutual respectful agreements. Children love doing and watching teacher impersonations! And the teachers get a kick out of it too!

- *Jokes.* Another common activity that children enjoy is telling jokes. The leaders explain that jokes must be appropriate for all ages of children in the room. Children love telling and listening to jokes. The older children

are often entertained simply by listening to the younger children laugh at jokes that the middle-schoolers clearly deem as ridiculous and not a bit funny!
- *Who Am I?* Each month a different class individually writes descriptions about themselves without writing their names on them, and posts the descriptions on a bulletin board available to everyone with the heading, "Who Am I?"

After the descriptions have been displayed for a couple of weeks, they are taken down and read by the assembly readers at the assembly. After each description is read, children who are not in the class that wrote the descriptions, raise their hands to guess who the person is.

Here is an example:

"I love tacos and hate ice cream. I have a sister, four fish, two cats, and a hamster. My favorite thing to do is play football. I love video games and Harry Potter. I have brown hair. Who am I?"

Sometimes the class running the assembly will come up with a random fun idea for the whole school to do together and you just have to go with it.

Here are some examples of those:

- *How many will fit?* How many boys can we can fit in the boys' bathroom at one time and how many girls in the school we can fit in the girls' bathroom at one time? Now this might sound a bit crazy, but we actually did this, teachers and all, and it was a great bonding experience. The older kids helped the younger ones; it required a lot of working together, strategy, communication skills, and so on.
- *All-school water play.* Get a few hoses, some squiggly attachments, water balloons, and everyone gets wet!
- *All-school freeze tag.* This works in a big open area. Once a person is tagged they have to remain frozen until another "untagged" player unfreezes them. Usually three or four children are the "taggers" at any one given time. Then you switch taggers, so other kids have a chance to be "it." If there are too many kids, you can break it up into smaller games of forty to fifty kids per game.
- *Obstacle course/relay.* Split the children up in teams with children of all ages on each team and have them do an obstacle course or a "popcorn relay" race. In a popcorn relay, children have to run and grab popcorn from one bucket and bring it to another bucket, trying to be the first team to fill their bucket; this can be a great bonding experience. These types of activities promote teamwork and communication skills. Children laugh, play, and encourage one another as they work toward a common goal. If some of the obstacle courses are particularly challenging, allowing an older student to go with a younger student is quite beneficial.

- *All-School Electives.* A six-week all-school elective, once per week, for an hour in the afternoon is a wonderful way for students to spend time together engaging in a fun activity.

One way it works is that two teachers offer an elective class that children are interested in. There can be any number of classes offered in any given session, depending on the number of teachers and students in the school.

Before deciding what to offer, you may wish to survey the students to find out which electives they are interested in. It is also important that teachers teach electives that they themselves are interested in.

Examples of electives include: cooking, mosaics, yoga, string art, ceramics, football/soccer skills, Dungeons and Dragons, community-service options, woodshop, and many others.

A list of the elective offerings is circulated to the classes and children sign up for three choices of electives they are interested in. Students are not always given their first choice elective, depending on the number of children desiring each class.

The elective class runs once per week for an hour, for six weeks. Children of all ages are in each class. This gives students an opportunity to work and interact with other children in the school that they normally do not get to spend time with. Furthermore, as the electives are taught by the teachers, it gives teachers an opportunity to interact with and get to know students who are not in their class.

On the seventh week, the whole school community gets together during the elective class time and spends the hour giving each group an opportunity to talk about what they did over the past six weeks and showing the school community what they produced if applicable.

- *Buddies.* Establishing relationships between older and younger students provides so many benefits to both that it is crucial to explore opportunities to develop these relationships and capitalize on them. Buddies is such an excellent opportunity.

Every kindergarten student who enters the school is paired with a sixth-grade student. The sixth-grader is responsible for assisting that child's transition into the school by being a "buddy" to the younger student.

Examples of things that older students do for their "buddies" include:

- Playing with them on the yard.
- Writing them letters or drawing pictures.
- Making them crafts, bracelets, and so on.
- Sitting with them at all school lunch, assemblies, and the school play.
- Helping them if they are sad, hurt, or upset.

- Often the sixth-grade class will get together with the kindergarten class once per month for a designated project like making play-dough, having ice cream, or reading books together.
- Going on a field trip to the pumpkin patch or other attraction together.

Other classes in the school can get together with one another as well, in a less formal way on a monthly basis. Second- and eighth-graders can have a picnic on the field together during lunch, for example. First-grade students would be thrilled to be read a story to by fifth-graders.

There are many ways for children to come together to interact and spend time getting to know each other in the school environment. These types of interactions are critical in establishing safe learning environments.

As children work and play together, having the opportunity to connect on a human level, they cannot help but feel camaraderie and compassion for these peers that they are spending time with, being vulnerable with and sharing their lives with. As a result, children themselves feel cared about, valued, and respected. These feelings promote behaviors of teamwork, empathy, self-regulation, and responsibility in the students, leaving no need or desire for them to bully one another.

Chapter Thirteen

School-Wide Rules and Understandings

In some ways, a school community is very much like a family. In my family, there was a family understanding that you don't wake my mom up on a given day before 10:00 a.m. In some families perhaps there is an understanding that you don't argue with dad, but you can argue with mom. Regardless of what they are, most families have some family understandings.

Schools should have them too. They may be called rules, and many of these understandings are indeed rules. However, they are not all hard, fast rules, and many of them are too abstract to be labeled rules. So we call them understandings.

One good thing about understandings is that the implication (and the reality) is that we all seem to agree on these understandings. I mean, nobody ever said not to wake my mom up before 10:00 a.m. in the morning. Even mom never said explicitly not to wake her, but we all learned very quickly that things didn't go too well when we did.

Sometimes these understandings come with an unspoken agreement. Other times, they are more clearly defined, as you will see.

The great thing about us all agreeing on them in a school setting is that many of these understandings were (and are) initiated by the children themselves and thus the children clearly comprehended the importance of these understandings. In these situations most students are highly invested in holding themselves and others accountable for behaving in accordance with them.

One of our school-wide understandings is *No Hitting*. This is more of a rule than an understanding. However, sometimes in the younger grades (kindergarten and first grade) children hit one another and we did not administer a severe consequence because they were just beginning to learn to control themselves and use their words when they are upset, rather than their hands or other body parts.

When hitting happens in the younger grades it is important that the child who hits is separated from other children, although not left alone.

Once he is calm, the teacher should help him talk to the child(ren) who he had the conflict with so that they can resolve their difficulty and discuss how he might handle the situation next time—generally using his words or asking for help.

Then the teacher should explain, in a calm voice without being angry at him, "We do not hit other people. When we hit children, then we are not able to play with children for a while. So, I am going to ask you to sit here with me for a few minutes. In a little while you can have another turn to play with kids."

After sitting for a while, the child should be given another opportunity to play. Usually the same child will not continue to hit children. (Remember, the class has already discussed classroom rules and that no hitting is always a classroom rule.)

If the same child does continue to hit other children at the kindergarten or first-grade level, after the third time he should be warned that the next time he hits another student, he will lose his turn to be at school for the remainder of the day.

When children are invested in the school program and love being at school, they do not want to miss school or be sent home. So at this point, if he does not have some other issue preventing him from controlling his behavior, he will most likely stop hitting. We probably sent a total of three children in kindergarten home for hitting in over fourteen years.

By the time students are in second grade, if they have been raised in a school environment where they have been supported not to hit one another, they should have a solid understanding of the fact that hitting is not an acceptable way of solving problems under any circumstances, as well as an ability to use other tools to solve problems.

As a result, children who hit at this age should immediately lose their turn to be at school for the remainder of that day.

We refer to this as "losing their turn" rather than "suspension" because losing one's turn to be at school for hitting a peer is a natural consequence, not a punishment. Children quickly learn that when they hit children, they lose the opportunity to be in the presence of children for a period of time.

The key to handling a hitting situation successfully lies within the adult's ability to effectively and calmly communicate these natural consequences to the hitter without conveying anger at her behavior. The adult's conversation with the child should proceed along these lines:

"Julie, I know you became very angry with Helen today when she grabbed the jump rope you wanted. However, you know that at our school, we do not hit one another for any reason. I'm glad that you and Helen had an opportunity to talk about your problem with your teacher.

However, when you get so angry at one of your classmates that you forget to use your words and you hit her, that tells me you need to spend some time away from other children. So for today you have lost your turn to finish the day at school and your mom is going to pick you up to take you home. Tomorrow is another day and we are looking forward to having you back at school tomorrow."

We also talk to the student about strategies for handling a situation next time they feel very angry, so that she does not hit someone again. She usually knows these strategies, but simply forgot to use them or chose not to in this situation.

This happens sometimes as we all make mistakes, which we also explain to the student. It is important to remain calm because children feel badly enough when they lose control and hurt another child. An adult dumping his or her feelings on top of the child's already upset feelings about her own behavior does not help the situation and only adds additional, unnecessary bad feelings.

When our school was rather young, we once had a boy who came to us in seventh grade. He was arguing one day with another boy on the yard when suddenly, another new middle-school student yelled out to him, "Hey, kick his ass dude, you don't get in trouble at this school!"

While this was true that students don't get in trouble, the natural consequence for hitting another student was being sent home from school because we could not have a child at school hurt other students, as this behavior threatens the safety of all students. So, call it what you will, the fact is that all students were held accountable for their actions. In this situation, fortunately a teacher stepped into the argument to assist the boys before it escalated.

It is crucial for the teacher to remain calm when handling these challenges between students. When an adult acts inappropriately it may backfire completely and instead of the child taking responsibility for his own behavior, he may simply focus on being angry at the adult who yelled, overreacted, and became furious with him. In this case you have lost an opportunity to help the child grow from owning and taking responsibility for her behavior.

This process of children losing their turn for the day for hitting sends a clear message to students that hitting is not acceptable and will not be tolerated. It works very well in the school environment with students from second grade and up.

Usually, however, as stated earlier, if a child has been at a school that supports a "no hitting" policy, by the time children are in second grade, they rarely resort to hitting. The main hitting problems occur with children who transfer into the school in the upper grades, third grade and up, from other schools that have not implemented this type of program.

ACCEPTANCE OF EVERYONE

Acceptance of Everyone is a very important all-school understanding that includes many categories. The reason this falls under the category of an understanding is because it is too abstract to be labeled a rule.

While hitting is very concrete, treating people well and accepting one another is something that needs to be discussed, modeled, and constantly addressed over time in the school environment in order to become understood by all children in the school community.

Acceptance of everyone means the following:

- We don't have to be friends with everyone, but we are kind to everyone.
- We treat everyone with respect.
- We don't tease anyone.
- We don't call people mean, hurtful, or insulting names, or any names that the person doesn't agree to be called.
- We don't make fun of people for any reason whatsoever.

As with all school rules and understandings, the earlier we begin to teach and model acceptance of everyone in the school environment, the easier it is to maintain throughout the school.

We had a new student enter the school in our second-grade class. One day the class was having a discussion and a girl raised her hand to add a comment to the discussion. After her comment, the new boy said, "Well that was a pretty stupid thing to say."

For a moment the children just looked at one another. After a little while, two or three children started to explain to the new boy that we don't talk to each other that way at our school.

This type of thing happened several times with the new boy during his first several weeks at school. At one point the children were pretty frustrated with him because of his hurtful behavior. The class ended up having a class chat about it. The new boy was able to explain to the class how he was treated at his past school, which, according to him, was roughly how he'd been treating kids at this new school.

The teacher helped explain to everyone that it might take a little while for the new boy to get used to how things are done differently at our school. The chat cleared the air and helped the new boy adjust more quickly.

Teasing, name-calling, insulting, or making fun of other people simply cannot be tolerated at school, or anywhere. When students discuss class rules this is always a rule they agree upon. If, for some reason, this rule is not brought up in the discussion about rules, the teacher should bring it up.

Sometimes a few students will say they don't mind being teased or insulted. If this happens, and they are not outvoted by the rest of the group, I suggest that you inform the class that there will be no teasing, name-calling, and so on at your school, as that is your school policy. Perhaps you can engage the kids in a discussion as to why they think this is your school policy.

While it's better if the kids come up with this rule by themselves, it's important enough to insist on even if they don't agree. If it's not your school policy yet, then you can have it be your classroom policy.

Treating others badly can take a variety of forms. Overt teasing and meanness is obvious and direct and is easier to detect and address. Subtle meanness, which is not as easy to see, or happens when adults are not around, can be more difficult to handle. Because these behaviors take a variety of different forms, there are many ways of dealing with them.

Chats, one-on-one discussions, problem-solving discussions with two or more children, and special time work well in helping children with these issues. This is assuming that the adults have made a connection with the students or students who are experiencing difficulties in these areas.

An important thing to remember in regard to helping children deal with teasing, name calling, and other hurtful behaviors is that there must be safe systems set up in the school environment to prevent these issues from occurring, providing support for children when the issues do occur, and ensuring follow-up communication after there has been a problem to provide closure and a feeling of safety for all involved.

CONSISTENCY IS REQUIRED

The reason many school-wide bullying programs have not proven effective is that they are implemented intermittently, rather than consistently over time, and are not an ongoing part of the school curriculum. As a result students are not being shown a model on a daily basis of how to think well of one another, treat each other kindly, and be friendly to all people.

How interesting that our schools wouldn't consider allowing students to go a day or two without studying history or science, but will allow months to fly by without the thought of teaching students how to be thoughtful and respectful toward each other!

It isn't enough simply not to tease, hurt, or insult other people. Accepting everyone includes being thoughtfully tolerant of one another's differences and challenges.

In one of our class chats the students were talking about problems in the class. Somebody brought up (in all seriousness) that Jim picks his nose and eats it, which, as was said, "really grosses me out." The other children agreed that they noticed this behavior as well and asked Jim to stop and he agreed to try.

At the next chat, when asked how Jim was doing with regard to working on this behavior, the kids stated that this was still happening. Jim said that he was doing it less, but that it was difficult for him to stop. The class talked about it for a while and realized that Jim felt he needed something in his mouth.

The children helped find a solution to something else Jim could put in his mouth during the day (gum) that the teacher agreed would be acceptable. This helped Jim to stop his annoying nose-picking behavior at school.

While it was difficult that Jim was the only child allowed to chew gum at school, the children were able to accept this because it helped alleviate Jim's undesirable behavior.

This may sound like an extremely tolerant and mature group of children. However, it was merely a third-grade class of students who grew up in a school community where they learned how to respect and help one another.

SPECIAL NEEDS KIDS

In any school environment there are children who have a variety of special or different needs. These may include physical impairments, speech difficulties, emotional and social issues, developmental delays, and so on. Oftentimes these children are targets of bullying, or at the very least, are excluded from playing with other children because they are different, slow, odd, and so on.

It is very important for these children *and* for the other children in the school that this type of segregation not be permitted. These children must be included in all aspects of the school environment just like any other child.

We had several children with speech impediments at our school. When they raised their hand to talk, sometimes they stuttered significantly. Or they started a sentence, then stopped, started again, and took as long as three minutes to finish their sentence. The teacher sat quietly and patiently, waiting for the child to finish talking, regardless of how long it took, providing the model for how students are supposed to act when a child with a speech problem is talking.

If another child interrupted the speech-impaired child before he was done speaking, the teacher would say, "Wait a minute. Sam isn't done yet. We are going to wait and give Sam his thinking time."

If a child made fun of Sam, that too was immediately and publicly addressed by asking Sam how he felt when the other child commented about the way he was speaking.

Children need to hear how their words and actions affect their peers. A child telling his peer that he feels hurt by what his peer said to him carries much more weight than a teacher telling a child not to be mean.

One time we had a class discussion with a high-functioning autistic child, Carla, who was upset because none of the girls wanted to play with her. When the class discussed this, the teacher found out that nobody wanted to play with Carla because she called people bad words. The kids agreed that they would play more often with Carla if she would stop calling them names.

Carla agreed to this but was not able to stop her behavior all at once. While she made progress over time, she still called them names quite often. The chats began to focus on the fact that behavior can improve over time if people are willing to work on it, but that doesn't mean that anyone will achieve perfect behavior right away.

Carla was willing to work on her behavior but was still having a hard time controlling her word choice in certain circumstances. The children knew Carla was a bit different, but that was never addressed, nor was it the issue.

The real issue, and the lesson to the children, was that we all have behaviors and places in our lives that we are working on. When we interact on a daily basis, we have the opportunity to see these areas that we each struggle with.

Rather than be mean, intolerant, or hurtful to one another, we can notice one another's hard places and try to accept and help each other, as we each work to make progress in the areas that are difficult for us.

In class, for example, a student may say, "I know I get angry and play rough sometimes. I've been working on that." Or the teacher might say, "Jake, I hear that you are upset with Nick for yelling at you. Remember, Nick is still working on using a tone of voice that people are more willing to listen to."

The greatest gift we give children by supporting them in this way is the knowledge and ability to accept the flaws in others, and in themselves, without judgment. Many of the children who left our kindergarten-through-eighth-grade school went on to high schools where they have interacted with students who did not have the advantage of being educated in this way.

They are often shocked by the amount of negativity, meanness, and harsh behavior they see between peers at their high schools, as well as the lack of acceptance, empathy, and tolerance many students have for one another.

SOME CHILDREN DON'T LIKE ONE ANOTHER

It is important to understand the fact that simply because students are in the same school, grade, or class does not mean they will become friends. It is disrespectful of students to try to push them to have friendships with everyone.

Trying to force relationships between children can also impede their internal ability to make their own choices about the people they want to spend time with. Nonetheless, there can be a fine line between not choosing to be friends with someone and excluding or treating that person badly.

In the next section I discuss the different forms of exclusion of peers. It may seem contradictory to advocate allowing students to choose their own friends while also requiring that they refrain from excluding any students from certain activities. While it is not actually a contradiction to allow both of these to occur, it does take support in helping students understand and accept the difference between not choosing to befriend certain people and excluding them.

We begin this process of teaching children the balance between being a friend to a peer and not excluding a peer who is not a friend, by acknowledging that all people are naturally attracted to certain people and may feel an aversion toward certain others. We explain that they do not have to have friendships with everyone, but they have to be respectful of everyone, whether they are your friends or not.

Like adults, children are often drawn to one another for a variety of different reasons. In the same way, they sometimes have a distinct aversion to certain peers. If the aversion is due to an argument, disagreement, or particular situation that can be discussed and resolved, then supporting those children with the necessary actions that need to occur will be helpful.

Sometimes, however, there is not a specific reason for this dislike. It simply exists between children and when asked about it they may either deny that they dislike that particular peer for fear of getting in trouble by admitting that they do not like someone, or will claim that they do not know why they don't like the person.

It is crucial to discuss with students the fact that it is normal for all people to have a range of feelings toward others. Engage students in a discussion about their own thoughts and feelings about their experiences with various personal relationships, as well as examples of times they really wanted to be friends with someone or someone wanted to be friends with them, but the other person wasn't interested.

Make sure you preface the conversation by explaining that children should not use one another's names during this discussion so that people are not singled out. Eliciting students' input about why they think people might be drawn to certain people and not drawn to others can be helpful in helping students not to personalize a situation in which someone does not want to be their friend.

Furthermore, it can assist them in dealing with this issue should they find themselves on either end of the dilemma.

We had a situation where two girls became close when they landed in the same fourth-grade class. Laura and Sasha were together on a daily basis for the first month of school. After that time, Sasha lost interest in spending time with Laura.

The teacher talked to the two girls about their relationship in order to ascertain whether there was a problem that needed to be addressed. Ultimately, Sasha privately admitted to the teacher that after getting to know Laura, she felt that Laura was not a person she'd like to be friends with. Unfortunately, Laura still was very interested in being Sasha's friend and was not sure why Sasha was no longer interested in spending time with her.

After speaking to both of the girls separately the teacher got the two of them together. Sasha explained to Laura that they had been spending a lot of time together and that she now wanted to spend time with some of her other friends. When asked by the teacher if she would spend some time hanging out with Laura, Sasha honestly replied that she wasn't sure if she would.

It is important to note that although Sasha admitted to the teacher that she really didn't want to be friends with Laura any longer, this is not something Sasha told Laura. While taking the necessary steps to take care of herself, the teacher helped Sasha understand the importance of not hurting another person (in this case, Laura) in the process. The teacher then spent some time with Laura discussing other options for relationships she could pursue.

EXCLUSION OF PEERS

Another common way that children mistreat other children is by exclusion. Exclusion can occur in a variety of forms.

The following are only some examples of ways in which children are commonly hurt by being excluded:

- Being excluded from playing with a group of children.

- Being excluded from sitting at lunch or recess with a particular group of children.
- Being excluded from being in an informal club created by students.
- Being excluded from a birthday party (especially when all the other students in the class were invited).

Some children are often more hurt by being excluded than they are by any other form of bullying or hurtful behavior. While many educators believe there is not much they can do in the school environment to force children to include one another, we found this not to be the case.

There are several things a school can do to alleviate the suffering that children experience from being excluded by peers. Schools can set up some school-wide understandings that address the issue of exclusion.

For example, one day when we were a rather new school, a group of fifth- and sixth-grade girls were eating lunch together. When two girls came to join them, one girl from the group said, "sgo," and she and one other girl got up and left the group.

This happened for a few days when finally a teacher saw the process and went over to ask about it. The other girls were upset and didn't know why the one girl always said "sgo" at a certain point and then the two of them always left.

We found out after some problem solving, that "sgo" was short for "let's go," and it was a signal from one girl to the other to get up and go sit by themselves whenever a certain girl joined the group.

Shortly after that time we developed a school-wide understanding that all children are allowed to sit with any and all other children at snack and lunch at all times. This meant that you don't have to go up and ask people if you can sit with them at lunch. You can sit with them if you want to.

If you do ask, they will say that you can. If they prefer that you don't sit with them, they will keep it to themselves. Everyone can sit wherever they want. If a child moves to be with someone she would rather sit with than the person who sat with her, then that person can move with her so they can all sit together.

Sometimes two people will say that they really want to have special time at lunch or alone time. Occasionally, we would allow this to happen, but most often we'd tell the two of them that if they want alone time, they should set up a play date after school. School is a time when all children are all together and we include everyone.

This understanding applied to kids playing together as well. Everyone was to be allowed to play on the yard with everyone else who is on the yard at that time. If four boys made up a chase game and another boy, or girl, wanted to join, the boys had to let that person join the game.

If a child came to the teacher complaining that he wasn't allowed to join a particular game, the teacher would walk over with that child to the group of children and help that child talk to the group, reminding them about our school understanding of including all students in our games.

STUDENT-GENERATED CLUBS

This understanding also extended to student-generated clubs. Kids are often creating their own clubs at school and many of these clubs are quite creative and innovative. Early on, as a newer school, we ran into several problems as children created clubs and spent hours arguing, crying, and complaining about who could join the club.

The fact that most of these clubs never lasted as long as the arguments about who was in them seemed lost on the kids, but it was quite draining for the teachers.

After a couple of years of nearly pulling our hair out over negotiating these arguments, the faculty came up with a school-wide understanding that students were welcome to continue to form appropriate clubs at school, as long as all children who wanted to be members of the club were welcome to participate at the same level as any other member.

If children did not agree to this, then they could form and run their own clubs outside of school, but could not conduct club business at school. This proved very effective in ceasing all exclusivity and upsets around club membership at school. As a result, many students formed clubs that were open to all who wanted to join.

Interestingly, probably because they had a choice, children didn't argue about membership. Knowing that they can be included if they want to, many students choose not to join the clubs that are available.

Examples of student-generated clubs that can be fun and successful at school are:

- Stuffed animals,
- Save the environment,
- Raise money for animal rights,
- Stamp/coin collecting,
- Knitting,
- Dance at lunch, and
- Book club.

Clubs that encourage participation in activities that are inconsistent with your school's philosophy would fall under the category of inappropriate for school.

Examples of such clubs may include:

- Pokémon, anime, or other character-based clubs. (These may not be inappropriate by nature; however, they may be exclusive in that children who do not have the ability to possess the necessary cards, equipment, action figures, etc. cannot be in the club.)
- Clubs based on physical characteristics (pretty girls club, hot boys club, etc.).
- Clubs based on social status (cool girls club, tough guys club).
- Clubs that encourage unhealthy lifestyles (junk food club, lazy kids club, rebels club).

BIRTHDAY-PARTY INVITATIONS

One of the most hurtful forms of exclusion that we saw children suffer from over the years was being excluded from an invitation to a peer's birthday party.

Several years ago there was a girl at our school who had a sleepover party. She invited all of the girls in the class, except for one. The girl who was excluded was extremely hurt and sad. Her parents were terribly upset and came to talk to me about it. They didn't know what to do. They weren't sure how to support and comfort her, and what to tell her the reason was that she was the only girl left out of the party.

Those parents eventually called the mother of the girl who was hosting the party to tell her how their daughter felt about not being invited. It was a big mess and it was remembered for many years thereafter.

Many people think that birthday parties are not a school issue because they don't happen during school hours. The problem is that because the children bring the repercussions of birthday-party fallout to school, teachers aren't going to get much work done unless they help the children deal with their feelings and the problems that surface with regard to birthday-party issues.

We had had many discussions in our classrooms about how children feel about being left out of birthday-party invitations. Here is the bottom line: nobody likes to be excluded.

At our school we developed the following policy about birthday parties:

If you are having a birthday party for your child please *choose one of these options:*

- Invite all children in the class.
- Invite all boys in the class.
- Invite all girls in the class.
- Invite a few kids *only* but do not invite everyone and exclude one or two children.

Parents mostly understood this policy and were happy to comply with it. Occasionally a parent has stated that a child should get to choose to spend her birthday however she wants to spend it, believing we should not put restrictions on who the child should spend her one special day of the year with.

Our response was we need to teach our children that we have a responsibility to treat people well and think well of our peers every day, even on our birthday.

ISSUES OF SEXUALITY/GENDER IDENTITY

Teasing, bullying, physically assaulting, and humiliating children because of their sexuality or gender identity has been a hot topic lately as these incidences have been on the rise in our schools. If we are to address this type of harassment that transpires from one student to another around issues of sexuality and gender identity, then we must talk to our students about issues at school.

The earlier these discussions begin, the better chance we have at helping students develop acceptance, tolerance, and open-mindedness about lifestyles that are different from their own.

In the early grades, discussions about different types of families can be helpful in introducing the idea that there is no such thing as one typical family. Children in the class should share about their families. Some may live with a mom and dad; others may live with grandparents, a mom only, two dads or two moms, or perhaps an aunt or uncle.

In every class there are always a variety of different living situations. Inviting some of the children's families in to discuss their family life, jobs, favorite foods, and so on is a great way to become familiar with different families' lifestyles.

Questions that children ask about anything of interest to them should be taken at face value and answered honestly. Young children are not biased and judgmental; they are simply curious about people who are different from them.

As children become familiar with the numerous varieties of different families in their school community, they learn that their peers' parents, although perhaps different in color, ethnicity, sexual orientation, biological relationship to one another, and so on, have the same goals and desires for their children as all parents have.

In the older grades it is crucial that we continue to talk to students about issues of sexuality and sexual orientation because children continue to receive information about these issues. This information, coming from a variety of sources, is not only sometimes inaccurate, but it can also cause children to develop negative and intolerant attitudes toward people of different sexual orientation.

Although many educators feel it is inappropriate to discuss issues of gender identity and sexual orientation in the classroom, it is important to remember that you are not actually discussing thoughts or opinions about what people's gender identity or sexual orientation should or should not be or why people have a certain identity or orientation or what your own sexual preference or orientation is.

You are discussing acceptance and tolerance of people who may be or think differently from one another. It is important to keep this in mind, and also to remind parents of this, should they ask why these conversations are occurring in class.

There are times in classroom situations where natural opportunities for discussions about gender identity or sexual orientation will present themselves. It is important to take advantage of these opportunities and to use them as teaching moments.

One day, for example, in our third-grade class, a boy called another boy "gay" during recess. After recess, the students came in the class and were talking amongst themselves about the incident. The teacher overheard the conversation and when all the kids sat down the teacher asked the students what had happened at recess.

Jason said, "Luke called me 'gay.'"

The teacher asked Jason how he felt about being called that name. Jason replied that he didn't know what it meant but that the other kids laughed. The teacher then asked how many children in the class knew what the word "gay" meant. About half the kids raised their hands.

Then the teacher asked Luke what he meant when he called Jason gay. Luke said he meant that Jason was happy. The teacher explained that happy is one meaning of the word gay but that it is not the meaning he believed Luke was referring to. (The teacher knew Luke well, had a solid relationship with him, and understood that Luke knew exactly what he had called Jason.)

The teacher again asked Luke to explain his meaning of gay. Luke then explained that it meant that a boy wanted to marry another boy and that he called Jason gay because Jason tried to hold his hand at recess.

This opened the door to a very productive classroom conversation in which the teacher was able to help students explore the following:

- How it feels to be teased and laughed at.
- Different names that may be used to refer to sexual preference or sexual orientation.
- Why people tease people who are homosexual (or different in other ways from themselves in the way they look, feel, or their beliefs).
- How it feels to students in the class who come from homosexual families or have friends who are homosexual when they hear children being called names or being teased about sexual preference or sexual orientation.
- What we can do when we hear this type of teasing or name calling (or any other type) at school or outside of school.

We have often had children transfer to our school from different schools in older grades, from fourth grade and up. These students had usually not been in schools where children had been supported to think well of one another and many of them throw around derogatory names and words without any thought whatsoever. For many children it is the norm to call someone a name or to refer to someone's behavior with an offensive term.

Once these new students learned that their behavior is not only considered uncool in our school environment, but it is also offensive and intolerable, they begin to learn new ways of talking and relating to their peers.

We had a new sixth-grade girl who was trying to be friendly. One day in class when the kids were talking about sexual orientation, she stated, "I like gay people. They are nice. As long as they don't bother me, I'm fine with them."

This was another great opening for a conversation in that classroom about the many thoughts and feelings the other students in the class had about that seemingly innocent-intended statement.

When discussions around issues of gender identity and sexual orientation do not occur naturally as in the previous examples, engaging students in third grade and older in discussions on the following topics will help facilitate conversations in the classroom that provide an opportunity to broach the issues of acceptance and tolerance around issues of sexuality and sexual orientation.

Topics of discussion should be chosen based on the age of the group:

- How is your family similar to or different from other people's families?
- What are some things that children tease or make fun of other children about? Make a list. Why do you think they tease them about these things?

- What are names that you have been called or heard other people called that have been the most hurtful to you? Why have these particular names been the most hurtful?
- Was there ever a time in your life when you were teased or made fun of for something you had no control over? What was it? How did you feel? What kind of things have you seen other kids being teased about that they had no control over?

As with all forms of teasing and bullying, the more we talk to students about issues of sexuality and sexual orientation, provide them with accurate information, and set the standard of behavioral expectation along the same lines of respect, tolerance, compassion, and safety for one another, the more we find that children are able to develop healthy, open-minded attitudes toward people of all sexual orientations.

NATURAL CONSEQUENCES

Natural consequences are simply occurrences that happen naturally as a result of a particular behavior. For example, if you walk outside in the rain without an umbrella, the natural consequence is that you will get wet. In a school setting, for example, the natural consequence of not doing any work in an Algebra class would be to receive a failing grade in the Algebra class.

The wonderful thing about natural consequences is that they are the natural result of your chosen actions, and thus leave little, if any, room for arguments regarding equitability or fairness of the consequence.

If a child steals another child's pencil holder and is then ordered to write one hundred instances of "I will not steal," it is not a natural consequence. It will likely improve the child's penmanship and remind him to be a little more careful next time he takes something that doesn't belong to him, but it is not a natural result of stealing.

A natural consequence of stealing would be to have the child who stole the pencil holder speak to the person he stole it from, let that person know that he stole it, and promise that he will replace it. He can ask the child where it was purchased so that he can try to buy the same pencil holder that he stole. Then the child who stole the pencil holder can let his parents know what he has done and how he is planning to rectify the situation. Perhaps he can earn the money to buy the pencil holder.

Natural consequences help children prepare for the realities of their current and future life by placing the responsibility of students actions on them. This sends the message to students that we expect them to take responsibility for themselves and their actions. In turn, children feel empowered by their ability to rectify their mistakes and they begin to learn the value of taking ownership for their actions.

Schools that help children learn to monitor their own behavior through the use of natural consequences rather than punishments empower students to make behavioral choices based on internal motivation and self-responsibility rather than on the fear of what will happen to them if they do or do not conduct themselves in a particular manner.

Several years ago we had a hot-lunch company that made these great-tasting round garlic rolls. Todd, a sixth-grader, thought it was great fun to stick the rolls in the toilets at lunch time. For a while we couldn't figure out why the toilets were getting stopped up and overflowing.

When we finally discovered what was happening, Todd was given the job of being the girls' and boys' restroom cleaner and monitor for two weeks. He had to check on all the restrooms at snack and lunch times, clean them up and report any problems to the office immediately. He also submitted a daily written report to the office. He was none too thrilled about venturing in to the girls' restroom twice every day, but he did complete his two-week duty.

Our toilets were not clogged up by anyone for the rest of that year.

Another year we had a younger class who made cookies one day to take to an elderly center as a community service project.

While the cookies were cooling in the kitchen, two girls from an older class came into the kitchen, saw them, and decided to eat several cookies. They were caught and brought to the class who made the cookies. They told the class what they had done.

They apologized and asked the class what they could do to make it up to them. The students talked about it and decided that the two girls should make another batch of cookies to replace the ones they had eaten. This way the class would have enough cookies to bring to their guests.

Here are a few other examples of natural consequences to behaviors that occur at school:

- *Writing on desks.* Wash writing off your desk. Then go around the class (and maybe other classes) to offer your services as the desk washer for anyone who needs desks washed.
- *Writing on bathroom or other school walls.* Repaint the walls.
- *Chewing gum in school.* Scrape gum off ground, desks, and tables for a given amount of time.
- *Talking and interrupting in class.* Step outside of the classroom until you feel ready to come back and be a part of what is going on in class, without disrupting others.

- *Not doing homework.* Do the homework on your own time at school during recess and/or lunch. If problem persists, homework must be done before student leaves school each day.

Chapter Fourteen

Cyber Bullying and the Role of Schools

Cyber bullying, which involves harassment by sending or posting hurtful images, messages, or threats via e-mail, instant messaging, Internet chat rooms, social sites, text messages, or by cell phone are all forms of bullying that are on the rise.

According to statistics from i-SAFE organization,[1] over half of adolescents and teens have been bullied online. Approximately the same number have engaged in cyber bullying. Furthermore, more than one in three young people have been threatened online and more than 25 percent of adolescents and teens have been repeatedly bullied via cell phone or on the Internet. Well over half of young people do not tell their parents when cyber bullying occurs.[2]

Cyber bullying raises numerous concerns for school officials as they struggle with the school's role on whether and how to address cyber bullying issues that do not occur on school grounds.

As local governments throughout the nation do not provide clear laws about off-campus cyber bullying, school administrators are often left to wrestle with how to protect student's rights for freedom of speech while prohibiting that freedom if it interferes with the right for other students to learn in a safe educational environment.

What is clear is that cyber bullying can be extremely harmful. Numerous cases of cyber bullying in recent years have revealed the painful, insidious nature of cyber bullying and the disastrous effects it has had on our children, including depression, isolation, and, in worst cases, suicide.

Part of the insidiousness of cyber bullying is that the victims may feel incapable of finding any relief from the bullying because not only can it occur continuously, as most of our youth are connected, wired, and communicating with one another constantly after school in the evenings and on weekends, but it is also difficult to detect.

Hence, cyber-bullied victims may spend numerous hours after school and the weekends, when they would normally seek respite from their tormentors, trying to deal with and combat bullies, often without seeking help from parents or other adults.

It is critical that educators address cyber bullying in the school environment, both in a preventative manner and if or when it happens to students in our schools.

Ideally, bullying-prevention strategies are implemented continuously from the time students enter the school. Then students will know, understand, and readily treat one another respectfully in most situations. Nonetheless, as we aim for progress and not perfection, we must be aware that for a variety of reasons, cyber bullying may occur in our schools even when we work hard to prevent it.

In an incident at our school, a middle-school student, Allen, posted a derogatory comment and picture of a peer, Roland, on a social networking site. The picture and comment spread and Roland was very upset about it, as were his parents.

Roland's parents came in to talk to me. They were worried about making a big deal out of the issue because they did not want Roland to be the one who "told on Allen and got him trouble," because they felt this would make matters worse for Roland.

It is quite common in situations like this that children do not want to tell about being bullied, in any form, because they fear repercussions when the perpetrator gets in trouble.

As discussed throughout the book, when the school community is set up to support students emotionally and socially, as well as cognitively, the students become aware that issues of bullying, along with any other social and emotional concerns, will be addressed when they occur.

It becomes natural and normal for students to discuss and resolve their relational problems in the designated forum depending on the situation. Not surprisingly, it is not unusual that a cyber-bullying issue would end up as a topic of discussion.

Additionally, when a school utilizes natural consequences rather than punishments, there is less fear that exists in the entire school community about getting in trouble. Students know they will be held responsible and accountable for their behavior, yet they also know that they will be treated fairly and with respect.

I had a long-standing relationship with Allen and had gained his respect over the years, so I called him in to discuss this with him privately.

After discussing this with Allen, I had a further discussion with the two boys together in which Roland was able to share his feelings about the situation directly with Allen. We discussed their relationship and how they planned to get along for the remainder of the year, in light of the fact that they were not friends.

Allen ended up apologizing to Roland when he saw how upset and hurt Roland was over the incident. We also discussed this incident with the class since both boys were in the same class and several students saw the photo and comment and had spoken to a teacher about it.

During the discussion in class, Roland was able to share his feelings of hurt, anger, and humiliation. Other students shared their thoughts and feelings as well.

Some kids thought it was funny and we discussed that too, asking, "Would it be funny if it was you in that photo with the comment?"

Allen listened to everyone, shared his owns thoughts, and he took the photo and comment off of the site. Allen and I had a talk with his parents about the incident.

While we are aware that Allen would not be happy about having to deal with this issue publicly, in class, part of the natural consequence of his action included speaking to his peers about it, as they were affected, and many of them upset, about this incident.

Although Allen was upset about Roland bringing this to the school's attention, Allen was hard-pressed to be angry or judgmental of Roland because it was not only Roland who was obviously offended, which Allen quickly learned when his peers shared their feelings about the issue.

I will not say that Allen and Roland became friends after this. They were never friends to begin with. However, Allen understood that he must maintain respectful and kind behavior toward Roland, and that under no circumstances would he be permitted to harass or bully Roland.

In addition to utilizing the other tools, skills, and activities discussed throughout the book, the following are some actions that may be helpful to schools in regard to preventing cyber bullying:

- *Student education.* Educating students about cyber safety is critical in today's world. A cyber expert may be brought into the school to discuss with students their use of technology, as well as the dangers technology presents and how to ensure their safety in the cyber world. It is critical for teachers to engage in dialogue with students about cyber safety and cyber bullying as they are relevant and important issues to all children.

- *Teacher education.* Cyber safety experts can also be beneficial in providing informative workshops for teachers regarding all aspects of cyber safety. Teachers can be educated not only about the extent and types of cyber use and cyber bullying, but also how to conduct dialogues with students about these topics. Furthermore, teachers should be instructed on how to ensure safe use of all school computers and cyber access.
- *Parent education.* Before spending money on hiring a cyber expert to come in and provide a workshop for our parents, I decided to ask our students about their own Internet use. My assumption was that being a small school with a lot of parent support and involvement, most of our student's Internet use at home was pretty well-monitored by adults.

I was wrong. I prefaced this question to students by informing them that I would like an honest answer to my question and that I would not use this information to get them into trouble with their parents. In speaking to one fourth/fifth-grade class, I learned that even students as young as ten years old were often left to their own devices for long periods of time, online.

One ten-year-old admitted Googling the words "naked woman." He was immediately led to numerous pictures of real-life naked women. Two fifth-grade girls admitted to looking together on the Internet, during a play date, at pornographic images.

My conversations with a number of students in various-age classrooms confirmed my belief that parents needed education about cyber safety.

- *Many parents are not as technologically savvy as their children.* While children of this new generation are born into the era of technology, many of their parents have limited or no knowledge of the cyber world.

Parent education must include a vast array of topics encompassing the different types and forms of cyber use, cyber safety, cyber bullying, parental-control blocking or filtering software, the legal ramifications of cyber bullying, and appropriate monitoring and use of technology in the home.

Parents can also learn how to communicate effectively with their children about cyber issues and what questions to ask their children in order to gain an understanding of what they are doing online.

- *Develop Clear Policies for Use of the School's Technological Resources, Including Cell Phones.* Like other school rules and policies, students and parents must be made aware of the guidelines for appropriate and acceptable technology use at school.

Once the school has determined these policies, hopefully by collaborating with the faculty, they should be discussed with the students and sent home to parents, along with the consequences students will incur if they violate the policies.

By taking the time to inform students and parents of the school's policies on the use of technological resources, the school sends a clear message to both students and parents that they are aware of and committed to the necessity of ensuring technological safety in their school community.

Specific cyber-bullying policies should also be included in the school's antibullying policy.

- *Keep documentation and evidence.* If parents or students report cyber bullying, administrators must document all reports (as with all bullying incidents). Additionally, if applicable, obtain printouts of any online bullying messages received from teachers, students, parents, or those you find on your own. If these incidents are ever reported to the police, it is likely the police will need probable cause and a warrant in order to search social networking sites and cell phones.
- *Let parents know that cyber bullying is a school issue.* One time I called a parent in to talk to her about her daughter who was cyber bullying another girl. The girl who reported this had brought in printouts of the cyber activity, which were quite derogatory.

After explaining the situation to the perpetrator's mother and showing her the printouts, she looked at me and asked, "Why is this your business? It happened off of the school grounds."

I explained that cyber bullying is a school issue because it affects the student's ability to feel safe at school. If students do not feel safe, they will not be able to engage themselves in their studies or in the school community.

Furthermore, cyber bullying affects not only the students being bullied, but all of the other students who see the bullying happening online and fear that they may become the next victims.

When students and parents are aware that cyber bullying will be dealt with at school, regardless of whether it occurred on school grounds, it not only reinforces the school's commitment to maintaining a safe environment for all students, but it may help prevent cases of cyber bullying, as perpetrators understand that they will have to face consequences for their actions.

This is particularly critical due to the unfortunate reality that some cyber bullies feel they are protected from being caught as they perpetuate cyber bullying away from the physical presence of others. There is often a naïve belief on their part that if nobody actually sees them cyber bullying, then they can deny having done it, especially if they create a fake name.

- *Utilize the experience of students.* While students often turn a deaf ear to adults, they are much more likely to listen to their peers. If certain students in the school have either been cyber bullied or have cyber bullied others, asking those students to share their experience with other students in the school can be quite powerful.

Older students can also be helpful in speaking to younger-aged students, as younger children often idolize their older peers, and are therefore receptive to their input and advice. Children often see adults as older people who don't have a realistic grasp on current social issues. They believe that their peers have a better understanding of the realistic life challenges they experience because they see their peers encountering and discussing social issues amongst themselves on a daily basis.

Preventing bullying is obviously most desirable and is a lot easier, on many levels, than intervening with bullying once it is occurring regularly in a school environment. Schools can go a long way toward the goal of preventing bullying by designing and implementing antibullying programs, such as those outlined in this book, and by implementing these tools, skills, and strategies into the school's daily curriculum.

NOTES

1. www.isafe.org.
2. drclaudiocerullo.com/2011/01/05.

Part VII—It's a Work in Progress

It is incredibly fulfilling to walk into a classroom of five- and six-year-olds and watch them play thoughtfully together, working out systems of sharing toys, helping one another when they fall or injure themselves, and using their words rather than their bodies to solve differences. It is also refreshing to stroll through the playground on any given day and not have to witness children being left out, teased, or made fun of by other children.

It would make sense that a school community that is able to put into practice all of these useful tools and skills discussed in the book would have no more bullying or social problems in their schools, right?

Wrong!

I was recently in a chat in our sixth-grade class where kids were discussing problems they were having with one another.

Nolan raised his hand and said, "Whenever I go to sit with Eric at lunch, he asks me why I am coming to sit with him, as if he doesn't want me there."

Eric's first response to this accusation was to deny that he ever said that to Nolan. However, several kids in the class quickly confirmed that they had been at the table and had heard Eric say this to Nolan on more than one occasion.

Both Eric and Nolan had been at our school since kindergarten and were well aware of our school-wide understanding about all kids being included in sitting with whoever they wish to sit with.

Once Eric was put in the hot seat by his peers, he admitted that he did indeed ask Nolan on several occasions why he was coming to sit with him.

The teacher then asked Eric why he didn't want Nolan to sit with him. Eric explained that Nolan chewed with his mouth open and spit food when he ate, which was very unappealing to Eric. Nolan told Eric that he would have preferred that Eric told him this directly so that he could be aware of it and work toward changing his eating habits, which Nolan then agreed to do.

By the time students have been practicing these skills for several years at a school that has a program in place and is committed to that program, one would think that episodes like the above would not occur any longer or that the above conversation would have occurred naturally between the two boys at the lunch table.

Unfortunately, that is not the case.

Wherever children are gathered for any length of time, conflicts, arguments, teasing, and various forms of bullying will occur. The critical factor is that we continue to address the issues promptly as they occur, and that we provide a regular forum for these issues to be discussed. All children resort to teasing, name-calling, excluding, and other hurtful behaviors at various times in their lives.

However, what we have found over the years is that we can greatly reduce these behaviors and help children learn to internalize other methods of dealing with their feelings if we constantly monitor the social climate in our classrooms, hallways, and playgrounds.

In the above scenario, on one hand, it is unfortunate that these two boys did not resolve their issue alone or with their peers at the lunch table. On the other hand, because they had both spent several years in an environment where they were taught and expected to think well of one another and to take responsibility for their actions, once the problem was disclosed in the open forum of the classroom, several beneficial things took place:

- Eric tried to lie but was set straight by his own friends, giving the message to all students that honesty is an important virtue.
- Eric then took responsibility and admitted that he treated Nolan badly and told Nolan why he did so.
- Nolan was given the opportunity to tell Eric how he felt about the way Eric treated him.
- Nolan also felt empowered because at eleven years old, he was able to understand how another child may not want to eat with someone who chewed with his mouth open and spit out food when he ate. Nolan readily offered to change this behavior, which Eric expressed gratitude for.
- The other children in the class witnessed the whole interaction and were able to benefit from witnessing the exchange and the outcome as well.

These types of interactions may happen several times during the course of one classroom chat because while children grow and interact daily, hurtful behaviors between them are bound to occur. As long as children have the time, space, skills, and support to work through these issues, they will be able to move past them in productive and healthy ways.

One year a while back, a new fifth-grade girl, Tracy, transferred to our school from her local public school. She constantly acted out in class by disrupting other students, calling children names, picking arguments, trying to start physical fights, refusing to do her work, and constantly complaining about having to attend our school.

It took us a couple of months, and a great deal of patience, to get to know Tracy and develop a relationship with her before she began to trust that we were on her side and were there to help her succeed. Slowly Tracy began to work on her behavioral issues and after several months made a great deal of progress.

While Tracy was able to curtail most of her offensive behavior toward the other students and even make some friends, she continued to refuse to do a lot of her work and to argue with the teachers.

As we learned more about Tracy, we discovered that her home life was pretty rough. Her parents, though together, fought constantly, and often physically, and she and her sister were often in the middle of these fights. We diligently worked with Tracy and tried to get help for her family as well, but were not effective at that. Tracy's rude and disruptive behavior was often brought up in class chats.

To her credit, Tracy felt connected enough to her peers so by sixth grade she came to care about how her behavior affected others, and she made a valid attempt to improve her behavior. However, having to endure daily trauma at home made it difficult for Tracy to turn her whole situation around and cease all of her negative behavior at school. Nonetheless, because Tracy stopped acting out against the other students, she was able to remain at our school.

While a lot of Tracy's behavior was still annoying and disruptive and she did not pass all of her classes, the other students learned to be patient, tolerant, and accepting of the fact that Tracy was trying very hard to improve her behavior.

We talked to the students often about working on particular behaviors and the fact that behaviors often take a while to change.

Just because teachers are aware and working with a child on a particular behavior, this does not mean that the behavior will immediately stop occurring. Our goal in working with any child must be first to protect the other children from being hurt physically or emotionally from the "offender's" behavior. When that is accomplished, we can then see if we are able to move the student who is behaving offensively to a place where we can reach her.

We can only begin to do this through making a connection with the offender and helping him to develop emotional safety at school so that he is willing to begin to experiment with making different, more effective behavioral choices.

The great news about helping students transform in this way is that the offender and the other children are able to witness wonderful and amazing changes in themselves and in their peer's behaviors over time. Children are able to see that if people are willing and are given the correct support, they can and do change.

This is an important and valuable lesson that will serve children well in school and for the rest of their lives.

Children also learn to be patient, accepting, and compassionate of one another's life circumstances. As they listen to their peers share feelings of hurt, sadness, and anger they begin to understand why some of these children tease, hit, and lash out at others.

One person's feelings do not ever justify hurting others, and we always must discuss this with the students; however, sometimes understanding where the behavior originated helps children empathize with a person who, until that moment, they were only able to see as mean or bad.

The following discouraging episode illuminated the fact that although we accomplished a lot of important work at our school in regard to establishing a safe environment, the insidiousness of bullying would continue to present new challenges, requiring ongoing attention and the perseverance of implementing additional strategies with our students.

Liam had entered our school after being kicked out of two previous schools. He came to us in sixth grade and had been held back a year in a previous school. Hence, he was a year older than his peers.

We worked with Liam on bullying issues that he initiated at our school. We closely monitored Liam, developed connections with him, and implemented many of the tools and skills discussed throughout this book. Liam eventually made several friends and exhibited a great amount of progress in regard to his bullying behavior. It was an ongoing project with Liam in attempting to help and monitor his behavior.

In the middle of his seventh-grade year, Liam's father took a job in another state and the family moved. After Liam left our school, we noticed subtle changes in some of the younger male students, particularly the fifth-grade boys.

Some of these boys began to wear different clothing. They laughed more often, appeared more relaxed, and were willing to interact with certain students that they previously didn't interact with.

After noticing this behavior for a few weeks, I sat down with several of these boys and discussed with them the things I had noticed about their recent behavior. I asked the boys why their behavior had changed.

Much to my dismay, the boys began to tell me that the difference in their behavior was due to the fact that Liam was no longer at the school. They readily explained that Liam made fun of them if they wore certain clothing and that Liam did not like a few specific kids. If these boys talked to or played with these kids, Liam chided them for doing so.

The boys further explained that Liam often threatened them if they told on him for any of his actions, and that he even physically hurt a few of them. In conclusion, the boys expressed their pleasure and relief about the fact that Liam had left the school.

In shock from this information, I asked the boys why they never reported this to an adult. The following are their responses:

- We knew the teachers would do something about it and we were afraid we would have to have a conversation with Liam about his behavior.
- We were afraid of Liam retaliating against us for telling on him.
- Liam was still nice to us some of the time. If we told on him, we were afraid he would be mean to us all of the time.
- We didn't feel like Liam's treatment of us was bad enough to where we weren't able to handle it ourselves.

After speaking to the boys, I was able to take their feedback to our faculty meeting, where we utilized this information in our future work with students and in handling bullying.

Although this information was upsetting for me to hear, it was critical in once again enlightening all of us to the work that must be improved upon and continued in regard to bullying prevention and intervention.

Furthermore, it reminded me that although we work hard in creating safe educational environments for children, the work is ongoing and will likely never be perfected. Yet, it is crucial that we continue to persevere, as our students have a right to be and to feel cognitively, emotionally, and physically safe at school.

THIS IS TOO TIME CONSUMING

I'm a runner and people often ask me how I am able to run twenty-five miles every week, or to run five miles at one time.

I did not wake up one day, jump out of bed and run five miles. I have been running for over twenty-five years. I started by running one block, worked my way to a half of a mile, then to one mile, and then up from there, over time. I ran for a limited amount of time, several days each week.

When I began, this meant running for maybe ten minutes, three or four times per week. After several weeks I increased to fifteen minutes, then to twenty, and so on.

Many people have explained to me over the years that they have tried to start a running program themselves but they couldn't keep it up for more than a few days.

When I pursue their explanation as to why they couldn't stick with their program, I inevitably hear stories about how they either went out and ran two miles on the first or second day and injured themselves, or they started by trying to run one mile on the first day and they survived, but after a few days of doing that, it was just too difficult and they gave up altogether.

The best advice I can give is easy does it when starting something new. It doesn't matter if it's an exercise program or the implementation of a bullying prevention curriculum—begin slowly.

The execution of the various skills, tools, and activities discussed throughout this book does not have to consume a large part of the time you spend with students in the classroom and/or in the greater school community.

You do not need to tackle all of the components immediately.

It took our school many years to include all of these aspects into our school community. We added different components slowly, over time. Furthermore, some tools and activities discussed in this book may be appropriate or relevant to some age groups or particular schools, but not to others. Use your faculty, staff, and administration to choose those that meet your school's needs.

It is a huge step to begin with the knowledge that as a faculty and staff you are committed to working together to create a cognitively, emotionally, and socially safe educational environment at your school. With that common goal you can begin to slowly utilize different components of the program on a daily basis.

Some of the daily components discussed in the book, which are designed to improve the overall feeling of safety in the classroom like teacher modeling, student problem solving issues, and so on, do not require any particular time commitment. Other components may be implemented on a daily, weekly, or monthly basis, as time permits.

The important thing to remember is that when students feel cognitively, emotionally, and socially safe at school, it is a lot easier for them to learn.

Although you may be taking some time out of your weekly schedule to implement nonacademic curriculum in your classrooms and schools, your students will be much more open and available to absorbing the academic information they are receiving, as they will not be distressed by various school-related social and emotional issues.

HOW REALISTIC IS THIS PROGRAM IN A LARGE-SCHOOL ENVIRONMENT?

This program has worked very well in a small-school environment where classes consist of twenty children or fewer and there is plenty of adult resources to assist with the variety of issues that occur in the midst of developing this type of school-wide atmosphere. How can we be sure that it will be effective or capable of being implemented in a larger school environment?

This is a legitimate and thoughtful question. While I cannot guarantee the effectiveness of this program in a larger school environment, I also cannot guarantee it in any other small-school environment. This is due to the fact that the effectiveness of the program does not and will not depend upon the number of students in the school. Rather, it will depend upon the number of committed adults.

I have hosted workshops where I trained several teachers who have then implemented many of these tools and activities in their own classrooms, without the support of their school's administration. They have had incredible individual and group success with children based solely on the work they have been able to accomplish themselves in their own classrooms in both larger public and private schools. Imagine how much more they could accomplish with more support!

This program can be implemented in any classroom community of ten students or of forty students. Granted, having a class chat with forty students, for example, will be a more lengthy ordeal than it would be with ten children. In this instance, you may have to set a timer and prioritize topics if you are unable to address all of the topics during the allotted time period.

Other components of the program may have to be altered as well, based on the size of the group. However, there are creative solutions to being able to work with all group sizes, big and small.

The most critical component is that students see and understand that the faculty and staff at their school is committed to providing them a cognitively, emotionally, and socially safe educational environment and that many policies, procedures, and actions are in place to make that happen.

Chapter Fifteen

Students Speak

In the research I conducted while writing this book, I found responses to many informational questions asked of students about their experiences of either being a bully or being bullied themselves.

Reading through several case studies, I found examples, stories, anecdotes, and discussions of children who had been subjected to every type of bullying imaginable. Some had tragic endings and others were much more hopeful.

In all of this research, while the horrific effect that bullying has on the lives of both the victims and perpetrators was illuminated, I found no informational material about students who have been educated, for a majority of their school years, in cognitively, emotionally, and socially safe educational environments.

As stated in the beginning of the book, I never set out to build a school that included bullying prevention. The ideas, strategies, and activities introduced throughout the book were implemented in order to provide what all children deserve—an educational environment where they are safe and comfortable to grow, develop, and learn. The fact that this type of an environment has additionally proven to prevent bullying is not surprising.

My point in addressing this is to convey the reality that many students (at our school, and at other schools that are working to prevent bullying) are being educated without the fear of bullying, and with the understanding that if it does occur, it will be immediately addressed.

The perspective of these children who have been educated with an alternative orientation and experience with regard to bullying can be beneficial in illuminating the positive difference an educational environment can have in assisting students to became aware, thoughtful, proactive citizens in the school communities.

The following are responses to several questions posed to students who were educated for several years in a school that implemented the program outlined in this book. All surveyed students have also attended other schools where this program was not implemented.

Note: The answers below are not actual quotes. In most cases, I talked with the students over the phone and took notes, and translated their words into the more workable language used here. Some of the older kids wrote and e-mailed me their response. I edited those mostly for length.

1. What do you feel are some important things you have learned as a result of being educated in a school environment where bullying prevention was implemented and addressed on a daily basis?

- Liorr, age seventeen, twelfth grade

Most importantly, I learned how to actually resolve conflict, not just brush it under the rug. Not only do I know how to resolve conflict, but I know how to express my emotions and always resort to talking rather than being silent or violent when upset.

These skills allow me to avoid severe disputes and have even led me to help my friends when they are having social problems. The social skills I've gained from being in a school environment in which bullying prevention was a priority will serve me for the rest of my life.

- Sofia, age eighteen, college freshman

I feel that I have learned respect for others. I also learned to be more compassionate rather that accepting bullying as something that "just happens" or simply assuming that "kids will be cruel." Bullying can be stopped and a safe environment can be achieved.

- Katie, age seventeen, eleventh grade

I learned that it is not only important to address bullying on a daily basis, either with your close friends or with bigger groups of people, but also that bullying can take place in many different shapes and all of them can be equally hurtful. Bullying is not just physical; it can be done by just saying one hurtful word or by not letting someone sit with you.

- Jenna, age twenty, college freshman

The most important thing I learned is that all people are different and we all have flaws, but we are all human beings and we must accept one another for who we are. I also learned that a person who is bullying has their own issues that have nothing to do with me, even though they may be trying to take those issues out on me.

Knowing that those problems belong to the person who is bullying, helped me to put that behavior in perspective and not worry so much about what others thought of me. In addition, being in an environment where I was safe allowed me to learn at my own pace without worrying about being judged by others.

One time, when I was in second grade, I was pretending to read a book. Since I couldn't really read yet, I was just looking at the words because I thought that I should be reading by then.

The teacher, knowing I couldn't read, came over and sat by me. She explained that it was okay that I wasn't yet reading and that everyone learns things in their own time. I remember feeling relieved after that about being accepted and not judged.

In what way do you think you are different from your peers who were educated in schools where bullying regularly occurred?

- Nora, age twelve, sixth grade

I think I'm more aware of bullying and how to stop it rather than being scared of it and letting it reoccur.

- Alyssa, age eighteen, college freshman

I am able to stand up for myself and others in situations where bullying or discrimination may take place, as I am aware of the severe impact these behaviors can have on a person.

Because I was raised in an environment where bullying behaviors were entirely unacceptable, I recognize them as such and am able to point out these behaviors to others, as well as to abstain from participating in them myself.

- Jonathan, age eleven, sixth grade

I am different in that I have learned to be myself rather than who other kids want me to be. At school I was able to be myself without worrying about being bullied or worrying about what other people would think of me.

- Will, age twelve, sixth grade

My peers who haven't been in this type of environment are not able to talk about their feelings or tell others if they are in pain. They just keep that pain to themselves.

- David, age fourteen, ninth grade

Any peers that I have that were bullied may not be as emotionally secure or they may deal with their irritation and anger in unproductive ways. I have become a more tolerant person as a result of this education. It's not that I do not feel irritation with kids; rather, it taught me a different way of expressing my irritation.

How do you translate what you know about treating all people with respect and dignity to your current educational environment if that school does not have a system in place to address bullying?

- Bryan, age ten, fourth grade

I try not to be mean to people and if other people are being mean, I try to help them. I try to use my words to help other kids.

- Kurt, age sixteen, tenth grade

I try to be friendly to everyone I meet. I try to give everyone a chance to be my friend. I have tried to get people not to bully others, but sometimes that backfires because I get associated with the person I am trying to defend and then the bullies start to bully me as well.

- Paradise, age fifteen, tenth grade

My current school doesn't have a bullying problem, but bullying is still present. When I first arrived at this school, most of my new friends would call each other or people they didn't like, "fags." I was always very quick to ask them why they would use that word. Eventually, they stopped saying it.

When I see or hear someone being bullied, not only do I help the kid who is being bullied, but I also ask the bully why they would disrespect someone like that.

- Madeline, age seventeen, twelfth grade

I try to use what I learned. For example, I learned to address problems directly with a person, using my words. However, at my new school, kids did not do that. Instead, they would tell an adult if they had a problem and the adult would punish the kid. I decided to address problems myself first and then ask a teacher to help me if I wasn't able to solve it myself.

Why do you think some children bully others?

- Talyn, age twelve, seventh grade

Sometimes the kid may be bullied at home or have other home issues and they take out their problems on other people.

- Tyler, age eleven, fifth grade

Some kids bully other kids because those kids do something or act different. I am helping with this at my school. I stand up to people who are picking on others.

- Ciel, age eight, third grade

Kids may bully others because they might think that if they don't bully someone, they won't have friends. Also, maybe something happened to the kids (who are bullying) and they take their anger out on someone else.

- Emmett, age twelve, seventh grade

Some kids don't even realize what they are doing when they bully others. When they do realize it, they think it is funny. Also, sometimes if kids don't know how to deal with any person who is different from them, they may bully that person.

What do you think is the most important thing for educators to do in order to create a school environment where children feel safe?

- Akwe, age ten, fifth grade

They should have a no-bullying policy at the school. Also having chats in the class was really helpful for me. It is also helpful when children feel they can talk to the teachers about their problems.

- Kayla, age fourteen, ninth grade

I think the educators should build a relationship with the kids so that kids feel comfortable with the adults. Right now I don't have a relationship with any of my teachers, so I don't talk to them about anything. I'm even kind of scared of some of them. Schools should not tolerate bullying. They should be set up where if kids are being bullied they can have a system in which they can work out their problems.

- Mac, age thirteen, eighth grade

Small class sizes and frequent class chats were very helpful for me. I also think it is helpful if kids are working with partners, for them to have a new and different partner in each activity so that it allows kids to build relationships with other kids that they may not have relationships with. Also, it is helpful for educators to develop relationships with the students so that students feel they can talk to them if they have a problem.

- Raymond, age eleven, fifth grade

Schools should have a lot of adult supervision to supervise the children in all activities—especially in the play yard. Also if a child is bullied, he should not be afraid to tell the teachers. When the teachers are told about a child being bullied, they should immediately help the child with the situation, and not wait a week before helping.

What do you think is most effective in helping children who are "bullies" and what is not effective?

- Beverly, age fifteen, tenth grade

I think schools can help kids who are bullying others by having an adult at the school form a relationship with the child to get to know what is going on in that child's life and why the child is bullying other kids. If the bully is having problems at home, or any other problems, and the teacher was aware of those problems, then the teacher would be better able to help the child overall.

What would not be helpful is to kick the bully out of the school because then the bully would just bully kids at the next school. It is also not helpful to embarrass or humiliate the bully because the bully will reflect those actions by doing them to other people.

- Kelsi, age twenty, college sophomore

I believe that the most effective way to help kids who are bullying others is to listen to their feelings instead of just punishing them for their behavior. School bullies are being mean and hurtful to others because they have been hurt themselves. Punishing school bullies by giving them detention or a time out does not actively address the problem and is not an effective solution.

In order to stop school bullies, parents and teachers must address the situation with understanding and compassion so that they can determine what is driving these children to purposely hurt others.

- Tommy, age eleven, sixth grade

The school should make sure that kids have a place to talk about any problems that are happening so they can try to fix the problems without having kids bully each other. What is not helpful is to yell at the kids who are bullying or to embarrass or hurt them in any way because this would just make the bullies mad and then they might start being mean or disrespectful to the teacher.

- Lilliana, age sixteen, eleventh grade

What is helpful is for the adults to talk to the bully to try to find out what is causing that person to bully others. What is going on in the bully's life that is painful? Then they can help the bully understand that the pain he or she is experiencing is similar to the pain that he or she is causing another person to feel by bullying that person.

They should also explain to the victim the reasons the bully is acting the way he or she does. The point is to help the two (or more) children relate to one another and to understand that they are both in pain.

OUR CHILDREN ARE WORTH IT!

As the issue of bullying has moved to the forefront in recent years, it has become impossible for our schools to ignore the disastrous effects of bullying behavior or to merely chalk this behavior up to natural childhood behavior. The quantity and quality of antibullying materials and research that have become available since 1996 has done a lot to shed necessary light on this very important issue.

As the materials and research have increased, so have the availability of bullying-intervention programs. While this is hopeful and is definitely a necessary step in the right direction, it would seem to make greater sense to strive for "prevention" rather than "intervention" in regard to bullying.

My hope and goal in writing this book is that parents, educators, and mental health professionals are able to see that there is a whole lot that we can do to create safer educational environments for our children, *before* they have to endure the horrific process of being victimized by bullying.

Our children are our future. There is not and nor should there be a more important resource to all of us than our children. Ensuring that all children are able to be educated on a daily basis in cognitively, emotionally, and socially safe educational environments is not something we should provide for them, it is something that we are obligated to provide, for all of our children.

It is something we can and must do if we work together.

Appendix 1

INTRODUCTORY ACTIVITIES FOR FACULTY/STAFF

It is important that school faculty and staff get to know each other and form connections as soon as possible. Here are some activities that will help that process.

Partner Interviews

Two staff members interview one another and then introduce each other to the group. Questions may vary. Typical questions include:

- Where did you and your family grow up? Tells us about your mom, your dad, your siblings.
- What is a positive or negative school experience that affected you?
- What is your favorite type of food?
- What is something you hope to accomplish before you die?
- Who are your heroes? Why?
- What do you do when you feel down or are having a bad day?
- Why did you become a teacher (or whatever your job is)?
- What do you like most about your life currently?
- What is something you would change about your life or that you are trying to change?
- What are some goals you have for yourself this year both personally and professionally?

Getting to Know Everyone

Form two concentric circles with partners facing each other. When I say "speak," you will speak to your partner on the topic I give you for two minutes. When I say "switch," your partner will speak on the same topic for two minutes. Then I will say "stop talking"; do so even if you are in the middle of a sentence. Next, the entire outer circle will move one space to the right. At the signal, partners will begin speaking again and the pattern repeats until every pair has spoken to each other.

- Who are you as a person?
- Favorite subject in school when you were a kid and why?
- Favorite things to do in your free time?
- Something you love about your family either growing up or current family?
- Why you came to this school?
- Things you liked and disliked most about school growing up?
- Most influential person in your life to date and why?
- Best trip you've ever taken. Where was it? Why was it great?
- Something you've never done but hope to do before you die?
- Talk about a fear that you have. Any fear.

Photo Scavenger Hunt

Each team must try to bring back the following digital photos of places, people, or things on the scavenger list. They have one hour to complete this task and make it back to the starting place. Participants can go wherever they need to go, but they must stay together as a group and be back on time. Here are the photos they are taking:

- A human pyramid with at least seven people.
- A group photo with at least one homeless person.
- A group (or partial group) photo with a fast-food worker.
- A photo with an automobile and an auto repair worker or gas station employee.
- The funniest photo you can take.
- A photo of ten shoes only.
- The largest plant or tree you can find.
- The most relaxing place you can find.
- A group photo with an elderly person (over sixty).
- A photo of something or someone naked.

Creative Community Service

Time allotment: three hours start to finish

Requirement: Must take digital photos of your experience and print out photos to share with group.

- Eat lunch together in a restaurant in the city you are in that none of you have ever eaten in before—cannot be a "chain" food or any other restaurant that has more than *one* location.

During lunch, as a group, you will decide upon a community service project that your group will undertake in the next couple of hours that you have together. Your project must be conducted in the city your school is in. You don't have a lot of time and you must use your own resources, financial and otherwise, although you are welcome to use any materials at your school that you may need.

Be creative, innovative. Think outside the box. There are MANY things you can do in two hours. Your goal is to complete some sort of project that serves any part of the community in some way, in the next couple of hours. You must stay together as a group and everyone must participate. Print your photos and meet at school by the allotted time.

Appendix 2

EMOTIONAL SAFETY IN THE CLASSROOM AND SCHOOL COMMUNITY

In order to enable students to learn in an environment free of fear, insecurity and isolation, we have to begin by setting up classrooms and school communities where children are encouraged to:

- Be listened to by the adults and the other students.
- Share their thoughts and feelings without being criticized, laughed at, or put down.
- Listen to others with an open mind.
- Understand differences and develop compassion, empathy, and respect for those who think and feel differently than themselves.
- Problem solve by learning to take ownership of their feelings, state their upsets in a nonattacking manner, be willing to hear their peers' upset feelings, and take responsibility for their own actions. The goal is to help children learn to be able to solve problems without needing the help of an adult.
- Feel connected to peers and adults.
- Be responsible members of the classroom community, as well as the school community.
- Have opportunities to work and play cooperatively.
- Experience natural consequences for their behavior, rather than punishments.

Teacher's Roles

Teachers have a huge role in establishing and maintaining safe schools. It literally can't be done without them. Here are some of the rolls they play:

- Help children by modeling how to speak respectfully to students.
- Don't criticize, put down, embarrass, or humiliate children.
- When children act out or misbehave, handle these situations without getting angry or speaking angrily to students.
- Facilitate problem-solving discussions. Be careful not to place blame or judgment, even if you feel a child acted inappropriately. Let the discussion come from the children, as children will hear much better if they hear from their peers as opposed to a teacher.
- Whenever speaking with young children, it is important to physically move down to their eye level. This shows children a level of respect. They are not forced to look up at you as an authority figure; you are just having a one-to-one human connection.

Tools to Utilize in Class

The following tools are also helpful to utilize with students, as age appropriate:

- *Student-centered problem solving.* When children speak angrily to other students, instead of the teacher telling the children not to speak to their peers in an angry manner, the teacher should go over and help the children discuss the interaction that just occurred. For example, saying, "Joe, I hear you talking in a loud voice to Scott. You sound upset. Can I help you talk to him in a voice that he will be better able to hear?"
- *Place attention on helping children understand their responsibility toward one another as caring human beings.* For instance, explaining issues as in this example: if a child is running toward the swings and accidentally runs into someone, explain that it isn't enough to just call out "sorry" as they keep running. Describe how the child should stop and acknowledge what happened and to determine if the person you ran into is okay and/or if the person needs ice, a bandage, and so on.
- *Student-generated classroom rules.* While there is always a need for a few teacher-generated rules, it is helpful to have a discussion with children about some of the rules the teacher feel are necessary in the classroom. The teacher can explain why there are rules about no teasing, talking in a thoughtful way to peers, working out a sharing agreement if two people have the same toy, no interrupting people when it is their turn to talk, no hitting, and so on.

- *Special time with students.* Have a sign-up sheet for students to reserve a special lunch-time with a teacher or administrator.
- *Allow students who are struggling to help do something special.* Teachers can ask them to help make a treat or to help set up an obstacle course for the other students in the class.
- *Classroom chats.* See part V of this book.
- *Role-play various problems seen in the class.* For example, if there is a lot of teasing going on, the teacher can split the kids into groups and ask each group to perform a role-play on how to deal with teasing. Each group can perform a productive way to deal with teasing and also a counterproductive way to deal with it.
- *Write, read, and discuss poetry and short stories.* Many issues like self-esteem, love and hatred, prejudice, and so on can be dealt with through poetry and short stories. Choose relevant poems and short stories that address the personal and group issues occurring in the classroom.
- *Whenever possible, use the curriculum to deal with classroom issues.* For example, in utilizing a study of social injustice and civil rights, have children create what they feel is the social hierarchy of the classroom. Ask the following questions: Where do you stand on this hierarchy? Who chooses the hierarchy? How do the people who are in power use their power in the classroom? In positive ways? Negative ways? What do we want our classroom hierarchy to look like?

Appendix 3

ADDITIONAL MIDDLE-SCHOOL CHAT TOPICS

In addition to the chat topic suggested in part V, the following questions have been used in middle-school class chats. Each question can be answered by all students in the class.

Another option is to write each question separately on a piece of paper, then fold the papers and put them in a bowl. Allow students to answer the question they pick randomly from the bowl as the bowl circulates the classroom.

It is important to implement these specific chats only after a significant amount of safety and closeness has been created in the classroom environment. Students will not answer questions honestly and vulnerably unless they feel safe in doing so. The class, as a whole, will not benefit from the experience unless safety exists.

I am providing a sample of questions from the following categories because these are the categories that we have found middle-school students have most frequently chosen to discuss, when given the option to choose:

- Personal Topics
- Drugs/Alcohol Use
- Relationships/Sexual Activity

Personal Questions

- If you could be anyone in the world other than yourself, who would you be and why? If you wish to remain yourself, give three good reasons why you would like to remain you.

- If you were going to die in two weeks and had to spend the last two weeks of your life with two or three people of your choice at a location of your choice doing *anything you want*, who would you choose, where would you be, what would you do? You cannot choose family members.
- Talk about something you would change about yourself if you could wave a magic wand and change one thing. It can be a situational issue, a personality trait, a fear or phobia. What would you change? Why? It cannot be a physical trait.
- Describe the ideal person you would like to be in a friendship with. What qualities would be most important? What type of person would you definitely not want to have as a friend?
- What is the craziest, silliest, or most insane thing you ever did? Who were you with? Are you embarrassed about it now?
- Would you say that you are the type of person who would honestly tell a person how you feel if they said something mean to you or to someone else? If so, how do you find the courage to do this? If not, what gets in the way of you doing this? What do you do in this situation?
- Do you care about what others think of you? Why or why not? Who do you care about how they think or feel about you?
- Talk about what you believe to be one of the things you love most about yourself. Describe why you love that trait, characteristic, attribute. It cannot be a physical attribute.
- Talk about one of your greatest fears. What is it? Why does it exist? What would you have to do in order to let it go?
- What is something you have done in your life that you are extremely proud of? Why were you so proud of this?
- Talk about something you have done in your life that you regretted doing. What happened? Why did you do it? What would you have liked to have done differently?
- Tell us something about yourself that nobody knows. What is it? Why have you not shared it with anyone yet?
- Tell us two reasons that you hate or love your life right now. What are the reasons? What do you do to contribute to them? If you hate your life, how can you change it?
- What do you feel is the most difficult part of growing up in your family? How do you deal with it? What would you advise someone if they were challenged with the same thing?
- Which of the following feelings is most difficult for you to experience:

  anger
  depression
  sadness
  fear

loneliness
frustration
any other you can think of

Why do you think it is so difficult? How is this emotion handled in your family?

Questions Related to Drugs/Alcohol

- How do you feel about experimenting with alcohol and drugs? Do you feel like it is something that you might want to try? If so, at what age? If not, why are you not interested?
- Have you ever experimented with drugs or alcohol? What has your experience been? Why or why not have you chosen this?
- Do you think there is anything wrong with kids drinking alcohol or experimenting a little bit with drugs as long as they don't overdo it? If not, then why do you think people try to stop kids from drinking and using drugs? If you do think it is wrong, what are your reasons?
- Are you the type of person who will probably enjoy some sort of drug use at parties? Or are you more likely to stay away from it altogether? What will influence this decision?
- Why do you think that drug and alcohol conversations are so interesting to kids? I mean, what is it, do you think that kids really want to know or to discuss about these issues?
- If you were with two of your very best friends and they got some marijuana and decided to smoke it, do you think you would smoke it with them? Why or why not?
- Why do you think some kids who drink alcohol and use drugs are thought to be the cool or popular kids?
- What do you think is fun and exciting to some kids about drinking and using drugs?

Questions Related to Relationships/Sexual Activity

Note: These questions may not be appropriate for all school environments, depending on school rules and policies.

- At what age do you feel you are or will be ready to be involved in a romantic relationship? What do you feel determines this readiness?
- What do you feel is appropriate for kids your age to do when they are involved in a romantic relationship? For example, dating, hanging out, kissing, and so on.

- Are you currently in a romantic relationship with someone? What does it mean to you to be involved with someone in this way? If not, do you wish to be in a romantic relationship? Why or why not?
- What is the most challenging thing about liking someone in a romantic way? How could someone get support with this challenge and/or learn to work through it?
- What is the most challenging thing about not wanting or not feeling ready to be romantically involved with someone? How could someone deal with this?
- How do you feel about kids between the ages of thirteen and seventeen experimenting with and engaging in sexual activity? Is it something you can see yourself choosing to do? Why or why not?
- Have you ever been sexually active with another person? If so, why did you make that choice? What do you feel about your choice now? If not, why not?
- Do you feel that students think differently, positively or negatively, about their middle-school peers who have engaged in any type of sexual activity? What do they think of or how do they judge those kids?
- What considerations will or do you think you will make before deciding to engage in sexual activity with someone?
- Do you talk to your parents about your thoughts/feelings about teenage sexual activity? Why or why not?
- Why do you think some kids are very open to experimenting with sexual activities and other kids are not open to it?

If safety has been developed in the classroom (including safety with the adults who are present), you may be able to ask children to raise their hands if they have been sexually active. Students who raise their hands can be asked if they want to share their experiences and their thoughts/feelings about these experiences.

Appendix 4

BULLYING-PREVENTION CURRICULUM

The following are rough guidelines for implementing the tools, strategies, and activities presented throughout the book. Goals and activities are broken down in order to help educators with curriculum planning and time management while incorporating these necessary and beneficial components into their schedules.

Topic: Establishing Safety in the Classroom (Weeks 1–6)

Regardless of their age, in order for children to be able to learn, they must feel physically and emotionally safe at school. All children need to feel important, valued, and heard. They must know that their thoughts and words are important and that they can share them without being criticized, ridiculed, or judged.

Children need to feel connected to their peers and teachers and to communicate openly and effectively with them. This type of communication promotes safety in the classroom and also paves the way for a more productive cognitive learning experience.

Goals:

- Students investigate themselves and others; learn about the elements of being human.
- Students become acquainted with one another.
- Students learn effective communication/listening skills.
- Students begin to form bonds with one another and with teachers.

- Students recognize their own biases and judgments and explore where those originate.
- Classroom policies/rules are discussed and developed.
- Physical, emotional, and cognitive safety is developed in the classroom.

Sample Activities:

These activities can range in time from ten minutes (quick game or challenge) to all day, and can be scheduled in advance to help with planning.

- Students each make a collage that they feel defines themselves. Any creative materials can be used.
- Various group games/challenges. See any games and activity book.
- Field trips. Day trips for younger classes and possibly a bonding overnight trip for older classes.
- Trust activities. Trust walks, trust falls, any other activity where students have to rely upon one another in some way.
- Truth or Silly circles. The class sits in a circle. Each person is given the option of answering any appropriate question asked by the person next to him. If he does not want to answer the question, he can choose to perform a silly task, chosen by that person. Silly activities must be appropriate. An example of a silly task is: run around the circle three times screaming, "I'm a crazy chicken!" Teachers should participate in this as well as children always enjoy watching the teacher do something silly!
- Group discussions, as topics arise in class.
- Write and read age-appropriate poems, lyrics, stories.

Topic: Diving In (Weeks 6–15)

As children begin to feel safe, they will often begin to let their guards down a bit and show their struggles more freely. This may result in kids experiencing various struggles with one another. Arguments and disagreements may occur; groups may begin to form and alienate certain kids; feelings get hurt; and so on.

We see this as a great opportunity to help children further develop their problem solving/communication skills and continue to work toward establishing and maintaining safety in class and at school.

Goals:

- Support children to handle their own feelings in a safe and productive manner.
- Support children to understand how to support their peers' feelings.

- Teach children the difference between feelings and thinking.
- Help children develop and use problem-solving skills.
- Help children develop empathy.
- Help children develop appreciation of the humanity of themselves and others.

Sample Activities:

Most of these activities range in time from thirty to sixty minutes. Many can be scheduled in advance, while others occur spontaneously, like problem-solving discussions.

- Active listening activities (vary depending on age).
- Problem-solving discussions (as problems arise).
- Scheduled chats on various topics, including the basic what's going well/what's not?
- Birthday appreciation circles.
- Role-playing activities on various topics depending on issues occurring in the class.
- Writing and sharing age appropriate poetry.
- Continuation of activities in weeks 1–6.

Topic: Progressing and Persevering (Weeks 6–Ongoing)

With good communication skills, trust, safety, and positive relationships established in the classroom, students continue to strengthen their bonds with one another and utilize their skills in the larger school community by engaging in various activities and experiences with other classrooms.

This helps to establish a close relationship between all students in the school community and provides an opportunity for older and younger students to interact, form relationships, support one another, and have fun together.

Goals:

- Provide opportunity for children to interact with other children of various ages.
- Promotes bonding of all school community.
- Provides opportunity for older students to mentor younger students.
- Provides younger students an opportunity to interact and engage on a regular basis with older children.
- Provides older students with the responsibility of serving as mentors and positive role models to younger students in the school.

- Helps all children in the school to feel they are valued members of a community.

Sample Activities:

These activities range in time from forty-five minutes to several hours and can be scheduled in advance to help with planning.

- Weekly or monthly Sings—all kids and parents come together. The students sing songs and discuss the events happening in their classrooms.
- All-school assemblies.
- All-school water play, freeze tag, or any big group game.
- All-school electives.
- All-school talent show—noncompetitive.
- All–school clean-up.
- All–school lunch.
- Other all school games/parties/dances.
- All-school community service projects.
- Buddies.
- Invite other classes in to see a skit your class performs or to see a project the class is working on.

Topic: Extra Enhancements (Throughout the Year)

These are skills/tools to be used throughout the school year to help with specific situations and/or general issues, depending on the needs of the group or an individual situation.

Goals:

- To meet a specific need of a child or children.
- To address a specified issue or problem.
- To support an individual.
- To address classroom social/emotional issues indirectly, yet effectively, through curriculum.

Sample Activities:

- Special Time with adult.
- Walk and Talk with peer to market.
- One-on-one listening time.

- Social/emotional issues dealt with through the curriculum. For example, during the study of the history of discrimination against various groups of people, the teacher can include activities and/or discussion about any discrimination students see in their classroom and school community. Why does this exist? What can we do about it?
- Checking in on a regular basis individually with your own students and with other students in the school just to make a connection with them.
- Adult mentoring an individual student who is struggling.

References

Bullying Statistics (2010). Info on Preventing Bullying, Harassment, Violence, Online Bullying, and School Bullies. www.bullyingstatistics.org/content/bullying-statistics-2010.html.

Bullying Suicide Statistics (n.d.). Bullycide: Teen Depression. www.teendepression.org/stats/bullying-suicide-statistics-bullycide/.

Castleberry, Kasie, and Mark Sanchez (2009). Make a Sound for a Voice Unheard. www.makebeatsnotbeatdowns.org/facts_new.html.

Claudio Cerullo (2011). Cyber Bullying Statistics. drclaudiocerullo.com/2011/01/05/cyber-bullying-statistics/.

Coloroso, Barbara (2008). *The Bully, the Bullied, and the Bystander.* New York: HarperCollins.

Hoover, J., and R. Oliver (1996). *Bullying Prevention Handbook: A Guide for Principals, Teachers, and Counselors.* Bloomington, IN: National Education Service.

Hartnig, Sarah (2010). Student Bullying on Increase, Federal Statistics Reveal. students.com.miami.edu/netreporting/.

Hymel, Shelley, and Susan Swearer (n.d.). Bullying: An Age-Old Problem That Needs New Solutions. www.education.com.

Lines, Dennis (2008). *The Bullies—Understanding Bullies and Bullying.* London: Jessica Kingsley Publishing.

Logsdon, Ann (2009). *Bullying in Schools—Recognizing School Bullying.* learningdisabilities.about.com/od/instructionalmaterials/p/serousbullies.html.

Milburn-Curtis, C. (2007). *How to Protect Your Child from Bullies: A Practical Guide for Parents.* Eversham, UK: Word4Word.

Olweus, Dan (1993). *Bullying at School: What We Know and What We Can Do.* Chichester, UK: Wiley-Blackwell.

Olweus, Dan, and Susan P. Limber (2007). What Is Bullying? Definition, Statistics and Information on Bullying. www.olweus.org/public/bullying.page.

Olweus, P. (1993). *Bullying at School: What We Know and What We Can Do.* Boston: Blackwell.

Rigby, Ken (2010). Bullying in Schools and What We Can Do about It. kenrigby.net/.

Shipp, Josh (2010). 3 Steps to Bully-Proof Your Kid. www.familyfirst.com.

Smith, P., D. Pepler, and K. Rigby (2004). *Bullying in Schools: How Successful Can Interventions Be?* Cambridge: Cambridge University Press.

Swearer, Susan, Dorothy Espelage, and Scott Napolitano (2009). *Bullying Prevention and Intervention: Realistic Strategies for Schools.* New York: Guildford.

Verma, Pawan (2008). Why Do Children Bully? www.child-discipline-with-love.com/why-do-children-bully.html.

Voors, W. (2000). *The Parents Book about Bullying: Changing the Course of Your Child's Life*. Center City, MN: Hazelden.

Young-Shin, Kim (2008). Bullying-Suicide Link Explored in New Study by Researchers at Yale. opac.yale.edu/news/article.aspx?id=5913.

Wipfler, Patty (1990). *Special Time*. Palo Alto, CA: Parents Leadership Institute.

www.ingramcontent.com/pod-product-compliance
Lightning Source LLC
Chambersburg PA
CBHW022015300426
44117CB00005B/201